Hiking Guide to the
Pedlar District
George Washington National Forest

POTOMAC APPALACHIAN TRAIL CLUB
Washington, D.C.
1990

Hiking Guide to the
Pedlar District
George Washington National Forest
by
Michael T. Shoemaker

Second Edition,
revised by author,
1990

Library of Congress Catalog Number 90-060908

ISBN 0-915-746-39-5
Copyright © 1981 by Potomac Appalachian Trail Club
1718 N Street, N.W.
Washington, D.C. 20036

**Cover photo: North Fork
of Buffalo River from
Mt. Pleasant**

DEDICATION

To my mother, a veteran PATCer.

ACKNOWLEDGMENTS

Kathy Hall, of the U.S. Forest Service, whose generous assistance included information and advice concerning the trails in the Pedlar District.

Norman J. Sykora, of Natural Bridge Appalachian Trail Club, whose invaluable directions for the Saddle Gap Trail trailhead enabled me to include that trail in this guide. He also alerted me to the planned construction of the Old Hotel Trail and provided information on the peregrine falcon release.

Bob Adkisson, of Tidewater Appalachian Trail Club, who alerted me to important changes in the White Rock Falls Trail, thus prompting me to rescout that trail.

Bob Young, of Potomac Appalachian Trail Club, who alerted me to the completion of the Old Hotel Trail.

Jean Golightly, of Potomac Appalachian Trail Club, who patiently supervised the publication of this edition.

ABBREVIATIONS

AT — Appalachian Trail
FDR — Forest Development Road
m. — mile or miles
Mt. — Mount
Mtn. — Mountain
PATC — Potomac Appalachian Trail Club

Table of Contents

Dedication iii
Acknowledgments iii
Abbreviations iii
Table of Contents iv
Preface to the Second Edition 1
Disclaimer Notice 4
How to Use this Guide 5
Hiking in the Pedlar District 7
History of the Pedlar District 13
Place Names in the Pedlar District 19
Geology of the Pedlar District 27
Flora and Fauna of the Pedlar District 31
Trail Descriptions
    FDR-162 33
    FDR-162A 35
    Bald Mountain Trail 35
    Mine Bank Trail 36
    Saint Marys River Trail 37
    Saint Marys River Waterfall Trail 40
    Cellar Mountain Trail 40
    Kennedy Ridge Trail 42
    Torry Ridge Trail 43
    Mills Creek Trail 44
    The Slacks Trail 46
    White Rock Falls Trail 47
    Sherando Lake Access 49
    White Rock Gap Trail 49
    Upper Lake Trail 50
    Stony Hill Loop Trail 51
    Blue Loop Trail 51
    Lakeside Trail 52
    Cliff Trail 53
    Mau-Har Trail 53
    Crabtree Falls Trail 54
    Fish Hatchery Trail 57
    Spy Rock Trail 57
    Railroad Trail (FDR-246) 58

King Creek Trail	60
FDR-48	61
Piney River Trail (FDR-63A)	62
FDR-1167	62
Pompey Mtn.-Mt. Pleasant Loop	64
Mt. Pleasant Spur Trail	66
FDR-51	66
Old Hotel Trail	67
FDR-520 (Buck Mtn. Road)	69
Staton's Falls	70
Panther Falls	71
Robert's Creek Cemetery	71
Elephant Mountain Trail System	73
Reservoir Hollow Trail	74
Elephant Mountain Trail	75
Indian Gap Trail	75
Indian Rocks Trail	77
Dancing Creek-Brown's Creek Trail	77
Belle Cove Trail	79
Rocky Row Trail	81
Saddle Gap Trail	82
Peavine Mountain Trail	84
Otter Creek Trail System	86
Otter Creek Trail	86
Canal Lock Trail	88
Trail of the Trees	88
Otter Lake Loop Trail	89

Westward view from Spy Rock

Preface to the Second Edition

Like a reunion with an old friend, returning to the Pedlar District after an eight-year absence was a great joy to me. This old friend has, of course, changed over the years, with some changes being for the better, and some for the worse. When I scouted and wrote the first edition of this guide in the summer of 1980, the condition of many of the Forest Service roads and trails, and the general lack of parking, made visits to the area a more rugged undertaking than today. For example, a visitor to Staton's Falls formerly had to park half on and half off the road, and hope not to get stuck in a rut or hit by a passing car. Now an excellent parking area allows visitors to enjoy the falls without worrying about their cars. The Forest Service has made similar improvements at the foot of Saint Marys River Trail and Belle Cove, and has upgraded both the parking at Hog Camp Gap and the road to it. The trail conditions have improved also, and most Forest Service trails now appear to be well maintained.

Observing the regeneration of the forest in a number of areas has given me some wondrous and heartening moments. The most remarkable transformation has occurred on the first few miles of the Railroad Trail. Formerly barren, exposed to the sun, and rather unappealing, this old railroad bed and logging road now supports an abundant growth of blackberry and saplings (some more than ten feet high), which are rapidly narrowing the road into a path. A similar magic, effected by a ban on camping at the site, has restored a carpet of greenery to the creek flats below Panther Falls. And on Big Levels, the rerouting of FDR-162 away from Green Pond has created the plateau's finest campsite in the clearing of the former road, now barely recognizable in its new verdancy.

New growth has not been entirely a blessing, however. The regeneration of trees on the slopes of Tar Jacket Ridge has obliterated acres of superb wild strawberries and has greatly diminished the interesting character of Hog Camp Gap.

The Pedlar District has gained two well-placed shelters in recent years, Cowcamp Gap Shelter and Elk Pond Memorial Shelter (a.k.a., Seeley Woodsworth Shelter). It has also lost one, Wiggins Spring Shelter, which was removed because its accessibility made it a favorite for wild parties that trashed the site.

The improvements, unfortunately, have also spawned their own drawbacks. Crabtree Falls, St. Marys River, Spy Rock, and the Cole (Cold) Mtn.-Pompey Mtn.-Mt. Pleasant area are attracting more hikers than ever. Anyone seeking solitude on a weekend is best advised to try such trails as Peavine Mtn., Belle Cove, or Rocky Row.

The worst change in the Pedlar District has resulted from extensive clear-cutting in the Peavine Mtn.-Terrapin Creek area. This timbering has wiped out, or changed into wide graveled roads, the following road-trails listed in the first edition of this guide: West Peavine Mtn. Trail, Terrapin Creek Loop, and Terrapin Creek-Peavine Mtn. Access Trail (still there, but now purposeless). In addition, the Little Piney River Trail has become so overgrown that it is no longer hikable. Altogether these total 13.5 miles of lost trails.

Fortunately, we have some new trails to compensate: Saddle Gap Trail, which creates a splendid new circuit; Old Hotel Trail, which not only creates a new circuit, but offers one of the grandest views in the Pedlar; FDR-1167, which overlaps a portion of the old Little Piney River Trail; and Elephant Mtn. Trail. These total 10.3 miles of new trails.

A number of name changes should also be noted. Since the East Peavine Mtn. Trail and Peavine Mtn. Summit Trail (as they were called in the first edition) now constitute the only good route to the top of Peavine Mtn., I have combined them and renamed them Peavine Mtn. Trail, an unofficial name created for the purpose of this guide. Other name changes have an official status. The portion of the old Indian Gap Trail that passes through Reservoir Hollow is now called Reservoir Hollow Trail. The first edition's Stony Run Trail is now part of the new official route of FDR-162, whose old northwestern end has been redesignated FDR-162A by the Forest

Service. Similarly, Va-635 within the Forest has become FDR-51, and Forest Service Road 1176 has been redesignated FDR-48.

The rescouting of trails for this revised edition was begun in May 1988, with the goal of 1989 publication. However, the necessity of preparing the 13th edition of *AT Guide #6* (Maryland and Northern Virginia) interrupted and delayed this work. Nevertheless, the information in this book remains current (camping fees, of course, are subject to change from year to year). The delay had the beneficial effect of enabling me to include the outstanding Old Hotel Trail, opened to the public in 1989 and scouted last September.

Additions and corrections are welcome and may be addressed to the author care of the PATC.

—Michael T. Shoemaker
February 17, 1990

DISCLAIMER NOTICE

Although the author and the PATC strive for accuracy and thoroughness in the material published, it is impossible to ensure that all the published information accurately describes the condition and location of trails and other features. Consequently, the author and the PATC and its agents expressly disclaim any liability for inaccuracies published in this guidebook.

The trails in this guide cross both public and private lands, the owners or administrators of which may alter trail conditions or impose regulations on the use of the trails. The author and the PATC and its agents expressly disclaim any liability for the negligence, wrongful actions or omissions of any landowner with respect to the trails, and of any trail users with respect to public or private property.

This guide and associated maps refer to springs as sources of water. The purity of water from any source cannot be guaranteed, and the author and the PATC and its agents expressly disclaim any liability for all impurities in such water. All water should be purified by boiling, but even this measure will not guarantee the safe use of such water, particularly if the water is chemically polluted. Creeks, rivers, ponds, and lakes should never be used as a water source.

The author and the PATC and its agents expressly disclaim any liability for the conditions of trails and other features described in this guide and for all occurrences on or at those trails and features.

How to Use this Guide

This guide does not cover the AT. Information about the AT is contained in *AT Guide #8* (Central and Southwest Virginia), available from the Appalachian Trail Conference, P.O. Box 807, Harpers Ferry, West Virginia 25425.

Except for the blazed trails and the Forest Development Roads, the trail names have been invented by the author. All of the unblazed trails are old unpaved roads, but few still carry any traffic. The presentation of the trail descriptions generally progresses from north to south and has been ordered to facilitate reference to adjacent trails.

The 1989 edition of PATC map #12 unfortunately bears no location coordinates. Rather than omit coordinates for the trails on that map, which would serve no purpose, I have retained the coordinates that refer to the 1981 edition of map #12 for the benefit of hikers who possess the older edition.

Two columns of numbers are given in the trail descriptions. The first column gives the distance for hikers proceeding in the same direction as the description. The second column gives the distance for hikers proceeding in the opposite direction. These numbers are complements that add up to the total distance of the trail. They can therefore be read as the distance traveled and the distance yet to go.

The direction of travel presented in the trail descriptions is the recommended, or most useful, direction. When hiking in the opposite direction of that which is described, references to left and right, and ascent and descent, must be reversed. In connection with traveling on the AT and the Blue Ridge Parkway, "south" and "north" refer to the general direction only, not to the literal direction.

Three degrees of steepness are generally distinguished in the trail descriptions: ascend, ascend steeply, and ascend very steeply. Three degrees have also been distinguished in describing the desirability of campsites: possible (relatively flat and smooth), good (an additional amenity, such as a scenic location), and excellent (first-rate amenities, usually including a water source). The listings of trees and flowers in the trail descriptions are for the purpose of indicating predominant, unusual, or beautiful varieties, but they are by no means comprehensive.

Forest Service Roads are now called Forest Development Roads, but the older term still appears on the PATC maps. The road numbers remain the same, except as noted in the preface. Two gaps in the Pedlar District bear nearly identical names: Salt Log Gap and Saltlog Gap.

Panther Falls

Hiking in the Pedlar District

This guide is not a substitute for common sense and experience. The author and the PATC cannot be held responsible for any accidents that may befall the hiker (see "Disclaimer Notice").

A third of the trails in this guide are unmarked. Some are subject to heavy growth during the spring and summer, and some are part of a vast labyrinth of old roads. The Peavine Mtn. Trail and Railroad Trail in particular cross such mazes, and one can become easily lost on them. Inexperienced hikers should stay on blazed trails.

The best maps to use are PATC maps #12 and #13. They can be obtained from: Potomac Appalachian Trail Club, 1718 N St., N.W., Washington, DC 20036.

Although 7½-minute topographic maps are essential to off-trail hikers who want to explore old back-roads, they are outdated and lack many recent trails. They can be obtained by mail from: Map Distribution, U.S. Geological Survey, Box 25286, Federal Center, Denver, Colorado 80225. They can also be bought over-the-counter at the U.S.G.S. headquarters (12201 Sunrise Valley Dr., Reston, VA) or at the Interior Department's Earth Sciences Information Center (18th & C St., N.W., Washington, DC). Topographic maps cost $2.50 each; add an extra $1 for postage-and-handling for mail orders under $10.

The ruggedness of the trails in the Pedlar District should not be underestimated. The many gneiss rockslides and fractured shale formations necessitate a sturdy hiking boot. The district is very dry in the summer, especially in the Big Levels area. Creeks and rivers throughout the district should be avoided as a water source, because most are polluted by oil, the result of a long history of logging and mining. Spring water should always be boiled before use; some Forest sources are contaminated with giardia organisms, which cannot be killed by chemical purification. Although several possible swimming and wading holes are noted in the trail descriptions, these places always present such dangers as snakes, sharp rocks, and slippery rocks. Hiking during hunting season (roughly October through December) and winter is very dangerous. Mountain peaks and ridges should be avoided in a thunderstorm. If caught in a thunderstorm, get away from your pack, lie low, and avoid high trees.

One should always be alert to the possibility of snakes. Carry a snakebite kit and know how to use it. Never put your hands or feet into places that cannot be seen. For instance, step on logs, not over them; and do not reach for blind ledges when scrambling over rocks. Snakes are apt to be found in the sun during the morning and in the shade during the heat of the day. Hiking alone is not recommended, and one should always leave a hike-plan with a friend or relative.

The watershed of Saint Marys River—including the Saint Marys River Trail, Mine Bank Trail, Bald Mtn. Trail, and Cellar Mtn. Trail—is one of the 15 designated wilderness areas in Virginia's national forests. This means that it is closed to commercial use and that roads and motorized vehicles and equipment are banned within its boundary. The old roads that already exist in the area will be allowed to revert to footpaths.

Similar, but less broad in its restrictions, is the Mt. Pleasant Special Management Area. Established in 1986, it comprises 5,900 acres in the Cole (Cold) Mtn.-Mt. Pleasant vicinity. Closed to commercial use, the area includes virgin hardwood on Little Cove Creek and a habitat for imported peregrine falcons.

Camping permits are not required. Camping is allowed wherever it does not impede the traffic on trails and roads, with the exception of the Crabtree Falls area (see description). Open fires are allowed, but are very hazardous. All trash must be carried out of the Forest; do not bury it. Feces and toilet paper should be buried with at least six inches of earth on top and away from any stream. At night, food should be hung ten feet off the ground and four feet from any branch.

Two non-commercial campgrounds are located in the area. The Otter Creek Campground, administered by the National Park Service, is open from May through October. A fee of $7.00 per site per night was charged in 1989. There is no fee after Labor Day. The Sherando Lake Campground, administered by the Forest Service, is the largest in George Washington National Forest. A fee of $8.00 per site per night, April 1 through November, was charged in 1989. Day use of the area costs $4 per vehicle from Memorial Day through Labor Day.

Eight shelters are located on the AT in the Pedlar District. Johns Hollow Shelter, located under a stand of hemlocks, is the best; perhaps because it is so isolated, it is completely free of mice.

The next nicest are Brown Mtn. Creek Shelter and Elk Pond Memorial Shelter (a.k.a. Seeley Woodsworth Shelter). Brown Mtn. Creek is very beautiful and features extensive remnants of a former community. The Brown Mtn. Creek Shelter is also fairly isolated since it can be reached only by a 1.8 m. hike. The Elk Pond Memorial Shelter is also nicely isolated and well situated on Elk Pond Mtn.

Although quite isolated, the Cowcamp Gap Shelter stands in one of the most popular areas in the district, so don't expect much privacy.

Similarly, the Priest Shelter stands near a very popular area, and requires only a 1.2 m. hike from the parking lot on Va-826.

The Harpers Creek Shelter is pleasant and isolated, but is occupied by bats.

The shelters at Punchbowl and Maupin Field can both be reached by dirt roads and are consequently popular sites for rowdy parties. Maupin Field Shelter is the dirtiest of all the shelters; in past years it was frequently visited by bears, though this has not been a problem recently.

The possibilities for circuit hikes are somewhat limited in the Pedlar District. The following are the principal possibilities.

One-Day Hikes:

1. From The Slacks overlook, The Slacks Trail (south), White Rock Gap Trail, White Rock Falls Trail—4.7 m.

2. Pompey Mtn.-Mt. Pleasant Loop and Spur Trail—5.1 m.

3. Reservoir Hollow Trail, Indian Gap Trail, Buena Vista streets—5.5 m.

4. From Hog Camp Gap, FDR-48, FDR-51, Old Hotel Trail, AT north over Cole (Cold) Mtn.—5.6 m.

5. Saddle Gap Trail, AT south over Big Rocky Row, Va-812 (quarry access road)—approximately 9.0 m.

6. From The Slacks overlook, The Slacks Trail (north), Torry Ridge Trail, Blue Loop (west side), road through campground, White Rock Gap Trail, White Rock Falls Trail—approximately 9.4 m.

7. FDR-520 and the AT over Bald Knob and Cole (Cold) Mtn.—10.1 m. starting from Hog Camp Gap; 12.0 m. starting from US-60.

8. Hike #4, plus AT north to Salt Log Gap, FDR-48 to Hog Camp Gap—10.6 m.

9. From Fork Mtn. overlook, Mine Bank Trail, Saint Marys River Trail, FDR-162, Bald Mtn. Trail—10.7 m.

10. Hike #4, plus Pompey Mtn.-Mt. Pleasant Loop and Spur Trail—10.7 m.

11. From Salt Log Gap, the AT south to Cole (Cold) Mtn. and back to Hog Camp Gap, Pompey Mtn.-Mt. Pleasant Loop and Spur Trail, FDR-48 back to Salt Log Gap—12.3 m.

12. The AT over Three Ridges, Mau-Har Trail—13.0 m. from Tye River; 13.6 m. from Reeds Gap.

13. Salt Log Gap to Spy Rock via the AT, and return by the Railroad Trail—approximately 14.1 m.

14. Torry Ridge Trail, FDR-162, Mills Creek Trail—14.5 m.

15. Saint Marys River Trail (including waterfall spur), FDR-162, FDR-162A, Cellar Mtn. Trail, FDR-42, FDR-41—16.4 m.

Two-Day Hikes:

16. FDR-162, FDR-42, and Kennedy Ridge Trail can be added to Hike #9 for a total of 22.8 m.; or they can be added to Hike #15 for a total of 27.2 m.

17. All the best views in the Pedlar District can be seen by combining Hike #11 and Hike #13 (26.4 m.); or by combining Hike #10, the AT north over Tar Jacket Ridge, Hike #13, FDR-48 (29.8 m.).

In addition, the following hikes are easily combined: #2 with #7, #14 with #6, #14 with #9, #15 with #9.

Three-Day Hikes:

Several are possible by combining the preceding possibilities.

Four-Day Hike:

It is possible to make a grand tour of all the interesting sights in the Big Levels area, with only 4.8 m. of repeated trail, in the following manner: From Mt. Torry Furnace, Torry Ridge Trail, Blue Loop (west side), White Rock Gap Trail, White Rock Falls Trail, The Slacks Trail (north side), Torry Ridge Trail, FDR-162, Bald Mtn. Trail, Mine Bank Trail, Saint Marys River Trail, FDR-162, FDR-162A, Cellar Mtn. Trail, FDR-42, FDR-41, Saint Marys River Trail (including waterfall spur), FDR-162, Mills Creek Trail, Torry Ridge Trail back to Furnace, for a total of 47.6 m.

The Pedlar District has eight peaks over 4,000 feet: Rocky Mtn. (4,072), Mt. Pleasant (4,071), The Priest (4,065), Bald Knob (4,059), Maintop Mtn. (4,040), Elk Pond Mtn. (4,034), Pompey Mtn. (4,032), and Cole (Cold) Mtn. (4,022). In my opinion, the following side trails are the most beautiful: Mau-Har, Crabtree Falls, Saint Marys River, Belle Cove, Old Hotel, Pompey Mtn.-Mt. Pleasant Loop and Spur, Mine Bank, White Rock Falls, and Bald Mtn.

The gates on FDR-42 and FDR-162 are open from April through December.

Overnight parking at overlooks on the Blue Ridge Parkway is allowed, but the Park Headquarters should be notified. Write to 625 First St. S.W., Roanoke, VA 24011.

In case of emergency, call the Pedlar Ranger District Headquarters at 703/261-6105 or 261-6106.

AT on Cole (Cold) Mountain

History of the Pedlar District

The Shenandoah valley and the surrounding mountains seem to have been a mixing bowl for many Indian tribes. The principal "native" tribes were the Cherokees, in Rockbridge County; the Shawnees, in Augusta County; the Monacans (or Tuscaroras), who had their main camp near Glasgow in 1670, and who dominated the northern bank of the James and all the land east of the Blue Ridge; and the Saponis, who used the greenstone of Long Mtn. to make tools and weapons. The principal "foreign" tribes were the Iroquois, from New York; and the Catawbas, from the Carolinas.

The Iroquois fought many wars against the Cherokees and Catawbas (who were allies), the Saponis, and the Monacans. The Saponis were virtually wiped out by the Iroquois, and the survivors migrated northward by 1740.

Arrowheads have been found in abundance in three areas: Elk Pond Mtn. (they can still be found along the AT here), the Spy Mtn. overlook on the Blue Ridge Parkway (collecting is prohibited), and near US-60 on the northern side of the Buffalo River (private land). These areas may have been favorite hunting grounds, or battle sites.

The history of the exploration and settlement of the Pedlar District vicinity presents two distinct stories. In the summer of 1716, Governor Spottswood led the first known expedition into the Shenandoah valley by crossing the Blue Ridge at Swift Run Gap. But migration from the east accounts for virtually none of the early settlement in the Shenandoah valley. This is because Scotch-Irish immigrants, moving south from Philadelphia, began to settle the upper Shenandoah valley at the same time settlers from the east were just reaching the eastern slopes of the Blue Ridge. In addition, the settlement of the Shenandoah valley proceeded more quickly than the settlement of the eastern foothills.

What the first settlers of the Shenandoah valley found there was a vast prairie. This prairie had been created by the Indians, who cleared the forest with fire, for the purpose of attracting grazing buffalo. Although the Indians had once inhabited the upper valley, they no longer lived there by the time the first settlers came. Instead, the valley served as a common hunting ground for several tribes. US-11 follows the route of the "Indian Trail," which was the major route of travel in the valley at the time of the first settlers.

Sometime between 1710 and 1720, a trader named Hughes established a station on the Amherst County side of the James River, a half-mile upstream from the mouth of Otter Creek. He was the first pioneer to settle in the vicinity of the Pedlar District.

West of the Blue Ridge, some Germans established a settlement at a site near Port Republic in 1726. One year later, a Tidewater company petitioned for 50,000 acres on the headwaters of the James. By 1732, the push southward had reached Staunton, where John Lewis and his family became the first settlers of Augusta County (which was then part of Orange County). Heavy settlement of the upper valley began in the autumn of 1737, and the first mill was built around 1740.

East of the Blue Ridge, Colonel William Mayo made the first survey of the area in 1728. Shortly afterward, Robert Davis established a plantation near the mouth of the Pedlar River.

During the 1730s, a settler named Waller owned much of the land around Piney River, Little Piney River, and the neighboring mountains. Waller had a mill on Indian Creek, near Lowesville, but it was short of water; so he built a stone dam and a three-mile flume to divert water from the upper part of Little Piney River. He was soon ordered to dismantle the dam because other mills on Little Piney River were being deprived of water.

A distinguished parson named Robert Rose made plantations in the Piedmont practical. He revolutionized the transportation of tobacco barrels (known as "hogsheads") by designing a dugout canoe that could carry them through the sometimes rough, narrow, or shallow channels of rivers like the Pedlar, Buffalo, and Tye. He was also the first to establish mountain pastures where his livestock could forage throughout the summer.

With 33,000 acres along the Tye and Piney Rivers, Rose was the biggest Piedmont landowner of his day. In 1739, he established his plantation, "Rose Isle," near Va-674 in Massie's Mill. He came west to reside on his plantation in 1747, and built a house, "Bear Garden," at the confluence of the Tye and Piney Rivers.

Rose was also an early explorer of the mountains. On December 6, 1749, Rose made an exploratory trip with John Blyre, a backwoodsman who lived in a cabin near a pond in the Montebello area, and Henry Bruch, who had done surveying for Rose.

They followed the north bank of the north fork of Piney River to Elk Pond Branch. Apparently, they took Elk Pond Branch and passed through the gap between Porter's Ridge and Elk Pond Mtn. They then camped near the headspring of Mill Creek. The next day, they backtracked to Piney River and followed it to its source, Lovingston Spring. They are the first known discoverers of Lovingston Spring. They camped near the spring and killed a bear during the night. On December 8, they followed the ridge of Rocky Mtn. southward, and then turned eastward at some unknown point. That night they camped by the headspring of the "South Branch of Piney River," which is known today as Little Piney River. On the fourth day of their trip, they went "across a mountain" (presumably Pompey Mtn.) and followed England Ridge down to Little Piney River, which they followed to Rose's home.

The first known fight between settlers and Indians west of the Blue Ridge occurred on December 18, 1742, near Balcony Falls, Glasgow. The Indians involved were some Iroquois who were traveling south to battle the Catawbas. Accounts differ as to who started the fight. When it was over, seventeen Indians and eight or nine militiamen were dead. The Indians fled, via the Blue Ridge, all the way to the Potomac. This battle triggered more conflicts between settlers and Indians, which led to the Treaty of Lancaster in 1744. The land west of the Blue Ridge had been Indian territory until this treaty, which ceded the Blue Ridge and Shenandoah valley to the settlers. Further conflicts with the Indians were limited to the western side of the valley. The French and Indian War of 1754, and the Pontiac War of 1763, had almost no effect on the Blue Ridge vicinity.

Augusta County was incorporated in 1745. With a population of 4,000, it was a thriving community compared to the still sparsely populated area east of the Blue Ridge. Nearly all the population of the valley was Presbyterian, and there were no stores in the upper valley until 1777. Staunton was surveyed in 1750, and was designated a town in 1761, the same year that Amherst County was created by a legislative act. In October 1777, Rockbridge County was established. Nelson County, formerly part of Albemarle County, was established in 1807.

The Pedlar District area was not involved in any of the major fighting of the American Revolution. When Tarleton made a raid on Charlottesville, on June 4, 1781, and nearly captured Thomas Jefferson, it was believed that he might continue to advance westward. People on both sides of the Blue Ridge flocked to defend Rockfish Gap, but Tarleton followed the Rivanna River southeastward instead. After the Revolution, many people emigrated from the Shenandoah valley to Kentucky and West Virginia.

The beginning of the nineteenth century saw the rise of heavy industry in the area. Iron mines near Buena Vista, Big Mary's Creek, Vesuvius, and Midvale supplied the many area furnaces. Grant's Furnace, built on Irish Creek in 1779, was the first furnace west of the Blue Ridge. It forged cannonballs during the American Revolution.

The Mt. Torry Furnace, a hot-blast, charcoal furnace, was built in 1804. It was owned during the Civil War by the Tredegar family, the great iron-mongers of the Confederacy. Destroyed by Duffie's Union raiders in June 1864, it was rebuilt in January 1865, and operated until 1884.

Cyrus McCormack, who invented the reaper on his farm near Steele's Tavern, formed a partnership with his father and John S. Black. They built the Cotopaxi Iron Works four miles north of Vesuvius in 1835, but the venture failed when the market slumped in 1839.

The famous Irish Creek tin mine lies 1.75 miles down Va-603 from Va-56, beyond the creek near Panther Run. The mine was in operation from 1855 to 1917. Government geologists studied the vein during World War II, but the mine was never reopened. The vein of tin is large, but because it is buried in granite, the cost of extraction is too high.

Until at least 1802, the only wagon road over the Blue Ridge in this area was at Rockfish Gap. In 1830, a lottery was authorized to raise money for the construction of a road from Lexington to New Glasgow, in Amherst County. This plan matured into one for a Lexington to Richmond road, and a survey was ordered in 1835. The road was built in a few years by Colonel John Jordan. The portion through the mountains is known today as Va-733, the Jordan Road, and US-60. Jordan (1777–1854) was a leading citizen of Lexington and the foremost industrialist of the valley. He also built Washington College (now Washington and Lee University) and helped build the James River-Kanawha Canal.

Work on the James River-Kanawha Canal was begun in 1831. The canal had reached Balcony Falls from Richmond by 1850. The section from Glasgow to Lexington was completed by 1860, but then the Civil War intervened. The planned link with the Kanawha River was never finished. After the Civil War, business conditions had changed, and the canal declined steadily. In September 1880, the Chesapeake and Ohio Railroad completed a freight branch that still runs the bank of the James. Named the Richmond and Allegheny Railroad, it links Clifton Forge with Richmond. The canal company went out of business soon afterward.

Mountain resorts and the medical faddism of mineral springs were very popular during the nineteenth century. The only such resort in the Pedlar District was Buffalo Springs, located at the Forks of Buffalo. It was linked to Lynchburg, Elon, and Pedlar Mills by the Buffalo Springs Stage Road, known today as Va-635. Built around 1800, Buffalo Springs was a great success until ruined by the Civil War. A resort was also planned for the summit of Cole (Cold) Mtn., but the construction was never begun.

No important battles of the Civil War occurred near the Pedlar District because it was too far south and west of the strategic geographical areas. During his valley campaign, in May 1862, Jackson used Rockfish Gap to secretly re-enter the valley and advance on the town of McDowell. After the battle of Piedmont, June 5, 1864, the Confederates retreated through Rockfish Gap. The Confederate wagon train, and many of the citizens of Staunton, retreated via the Tye River Gap. The wagons spent the evening of June 6–7 near the junction of Va-56 and the Blue Ridge Parkway. They remained encamped through the seventh and eighth, and descended to the east on the ninth. At the same time, Breckinridge came through Rockfish Gap from the east and pursued Hunter to Lexington. After burning Virginia Military Institute, in Lexington, Hunter attacked Lynchburg, where he was defeated by Early. Sheridan devastated the Shenandoah valley in the autumn of 1864; and in March 1865, he defeated the scant remnants of Early's army at Waynesboro.

A short-lived, speculative, real estate boom occurred in the Shenandoah valley in 1890. Buena Vista, incorporated in 1891, was planned and populated by a development company. The company soon folded, however, leaving the town in an unfinished, impoverished condition. Glasgow was also created by a development company, but it fared better because the Natural Bridge area already had a substantial population.

Because of their separate histories, antagonism long existed between the settlers on the east side and those on the west side of the Blue Ridge. According to legend, this antagonism spawned a feud, in the vicinity of Reed's Gap, between the Fitzgerald family, from the east, and the Coffey family, from the west. This legend is not confirmed by any known historical records. When a post office was established in the area, in 1897, it was named "Love" after Lovey Coffey, the postmaster's daughter.

George Washington National Forest was authorized by Congress in 1911, and was established in 1917 as Shenandoah National Forest. The name was changed in 1932 to avoid confusion with Shenandoah National Park. The potential purchase area is 1,740,014 acres, but this will never be realized because of the many towns in the area. The major unacquired areas in the Pedlar District, for example, are the Irish Creek and Tye River valleys, and the land between the AT and Va-151. The present area of the entire Forest is a little more than one million acres. New land is constantly being acquired, however, with top priority going to those parcels that fill areas already completely surrounded by the Forest boundary. The administration of the Forest is based on the "multiple-use principle." This means that the Forest Service tries to serve the interests of many groups. The Forest is used for timber cutting, mining, wildlife preservation, and recreation.

Additional historical information is contained in the following section.

Place Names in the Pedlar District

Place names are a repository for history. Most derive from physical description or personal names. Less frequently, the origin lies in a description that has some historical significance. Still fewer are the result of commemoration, or names derived from the "old country." Rarest of all are surviving examples of the many obscene names that the early hunters and explorers were fond of using.

The Indians who populated this area doubtless had their own place names, but few of these survive. The Appalachian Mountains are named for the Appalachies, a tribe in the southern section of the range. Shenandoah, which has been translated as "Daughter of the Stars," is actually a corruption of Sherando, the name of an Indian tribe. Other versions of this name are "Shenando" and "Sherundo." "Terrapin" and "hickory" are also Indian words that survive in the descriptive names of Terrapin Creek and Hickory Spring.

The oldest surviving, accurate map of this area was drawn in 1751 by Joshua Fry and Peter Jefferson. The following place names appear on it: Piney River, Pedlar River, Buffalo River, Tye River, Bald Friar, Priest Mtn., Three Ridge Mtn., Mt. Pleasant, and Laurence's Creek. It should not be assumed that these are the only established names of the time, nor that this is the earliest historical record of these names. The appearance of "Bald Friar" tells us that The Friar was once a bald mountain. "Bald Friar" and "Priest Mtn." also have significance in regard to a mystery to be discussed later. "Three Ridge Mtn." is a corruption of Three Ridged Mtn., which was the original name of Three Ridges. This map is the earliest appearance of Mt. Pleasant, and raises questions about the origin of that name.

"Laurence's Creek" is known today as Otter Creek. When and why this name was changed is unknown.

Descriptive names are generally the oldest in origin, having been invented by the early explorers, hunters, and surveyors. Some of these may well be translations of original Indian names. The Ledge, or The Blue Ledge, dating to about 1700, is probably the oldest of the non-Indian names. "Ledge" is an archaic form of "ridge." The Powhatan name for The Blue Ridge was "Quirauk." The Monacan Indians divided the range into three sections. "Cawasean" was north of Rockfish Gap, "Taweasus" was the area of the Pedlar District, and "Occanachie" was south of James River.

Some descriptive names are derived from physical features. A Fork Mtn. lies at the Buffalo River fork and at the Tye River fork. White Rock Gap refers to the abundant quartz found in the area. Green Pond is green from algae. Bald Mtn. (originally called "Bald Knob") is bald, having been cleared by fire by Indians who then used it as a signal station. Many hikers wonder why the heavily wooded Bald Knob was so named. The simple answer is that it was bald during the eighteenth century. Silver Peak refers to the appearance of this mountain in rain, rather than to any silver ore. Rocky Mtn., Long Mtn., Dark Hollow, Dismal Hollow, Three Ridges, and many others are self-explanatory.

Buffalo River, Elk Pond Mtn., Wolf Ridge, Panther Mtn., and Panther Falls are reminders of the time when all these animals were abundant here. (Mountain-lions were commonly called panthers.) Painter Mtn. probably refers to panthers, too, because "painter" is a common, early corruption of "panther."

Peavine Mtn., Grapevine Ridge, Chestnut Ridge, Piney River, and Piney Mtn. are examples of names derived from characteristic flora. Cashaw Creek might also fall into this category. It seems probable that "Cashaw" is a corruption of "Cashew." Sumac is part of the Cashew family of trees, and is in fact found in the Cashaw Creek area.

Another type of descriptive name is that which has some historical significance. Most common among these is Mill Creek.

Salt Log Gap, Licklog Springs Gap, Cowcamp Gap, and Hog Camp Gap all reflect a common practice of the eighteenth and nineteenth centuries. Most of the mountain land was owned by the lowland plantation owners. They let their cattle forage in the mountains all summer. When autumn came, they rounded up the cattle at the gaps. "Salt Log" and "Licklog" refer to the salt licks that were probably placed here.

Other historical-descriptive names that probably originated with the early settlers are Turkey Pen Ridge, Irish Creek, Whetstone Ridge, Swapping Camp Creek, and Twenty Minute Cliff. The fine-grain sandstone found on Whetstone Ridge was probably used by the early backwoodsmen for whetstones. It is a fact that Swapping Camp Creek took its name from an early trading post that was nearby. To this day, the people in the valley below Twenty Minute Cliff know when sundown is twenty minutes off by watching how the sunlight strikes the cliff at dusk.

Many historical-descriptive names are of more recent origin. The apparently authentic origin of Tarjacket Ridge is as unusual as the name. Sometime around the American Revolution, a man working on the mountain was caught in a thunderstorm. To escape the storm, he "runned off'n 'at mountin so fas' he tar his jacket." (See *Old Place Names, West Central Piedmont and Blue Ridge Mountains* by Alfred Percy, Percy Press, Madison Heights, Virginia, 1950.)

Wigwam Creek and Wigwam Mtn. are of later origin than one might think. Around 1800, some Cherokees wandered into Lexington seeking help. Many were suffering from smallpox. They were herded into the Irish Creek valley and quarantined in the area of Wigwam Creek. Some of their descendants still live in the area.

Yankee Horse Ridge and Spy Mtn. date to the Civil War. Legend says that a Union soldier was being chased along Yankee Horse Ridge when his horse died of exhaustion. Spy Mtn. was used as a lookout post by Union sympathizers who lived in some of the neighboring hollows. Whether or not Spy Rock has a similar origin is unknown.

Stillhouse Hollow was named for a legal distillery that once stood near the spring there.

Orebank Creek, Mine Bank Mtn., and Mine Bank Creek take their names from the many mines in the area. These probably date from the mid-to-late nineteenth century.

Several of the counties and towns in the Pedlar District vicinity have commemorative names, or take their names from places in the "old country." Augusta County was named for Princess Augusta, the mother of George III. Nelson County was named for General

Thomas Nelson, Jr., the third governor of Virginia. Amherst County was named for Colonel Jeffrey Amherst, a hero of the French and Indian War. Lexington took its name to commemorate the revolutionary battle of Lexington, and Waynesboro was named in honor of revolutionary hero "Mad" Anthony Wayne.

Cornwall, with its many mines nearby, was named for the mines of Cornwall, England.

Snowden was originally Waugh's Ferry, or Rope Ferry. Sometime in the 1880s a Welshman named Davis changed the name to Snowden, after Mt. Snowdon in Wales.

The Jordan family named one of their furnaces for the Mexican War battle of Buena Vista. The town of Buena Vista took its name from this furnace, which was five miles away.

Italian settlers named Naola and Vesuvius for an Italian town and volcano. Pompey Mtn. probably has a similar origin, but nothing is known about it.

Among the place names taken from personal names, those that derive from the early explorers and surveyors are the oldest and least numerous. Tye River was discovered in 1735 by Allen Tye, a famous explorer of the Blue Ridge, who eventually settled in Tennessee. Although peddlers were common along the Pedlar River, the river's name derives from the surname of an early settler who drowned in it. The name of the Pedlar River was in use at least as early as 1742. Floyd's Mtn. was probably named by John Floyd, an early explorer from Amherst County. Samuel Burks, a noted surveyor of the 1730s, probably named Burks Mtn. Robert Rose's diary, circa 1750, mentions his meeting a miner named "Netles," who lived in the vicinity of the present-day Nettle Creek. Cash Hollow is almost certainly named for Howard Cash, who surveyed the area for Robert Rose. Crabtree Creek and Falls were probably discovered and named by William Crabtree, a noted explorer who settled on the Holston River in 1777.

The origin of the name Lovingston Spring, discovered in 1749 by Robert Rose, Henry Bruch, and John Blyre, is a mystery. John Loving, an early settler, owned a plantation known as "Nassaw" on a tract of land between the Tye and Rockfish Rivers. The town of Lovingston, which is on this tract, is almost certainly named for him. It seems likely that there is some historical link between Lovingston Spring and the town of Lovingston.

Place names derived from personal names are most commonly those of early landowners. These originally took the possessive form, but the apostrophe (or both the apostrophe and the "s") is usually eliminated on modern maps. The mountains along the western edge of the Pedlar District (Lowry, Coleman, Paxton, Garnet, McClure, White, Coates, Adams, and McClung) are all named after prominent families of Lexington and Buena Vista. Staton's Creek was probably owned by William Staton of Amherst County, a prominent, early landowner. Fletcher Mtn. was owned by Elijah Fletcher, a wealthy, Amherst County plantation owner of the early 1800s. Campbell Creek, Maupin Field Shelter, and Reed's Gap (a corruption of "Reid's Gap") derive from old Nelson County surnames. The Jordan Road, Va-733, was built by John Jordan (1777–1854). Massie's Mill was founded by William E. Massie, Tyro was taken from the name of Massie's home, and Montebello was named for Massie's great-grandfather. Hite's, Taylor's, and Zink's hollows, near Spy Mtn., are named for Union sympathizers who hid in them during the Civil War. Clark's Gap is named for the character of a famous folk-song, "Ol' Joe Clark," which was written by San Downey, who lived on Irish Creek and was a wagon-driver for the South River Lumber Company.

A little-known category of place names is that of obscene names invented by the early backwoodsmen. Few examples of these have survived. Maintop Mtn. was originally named Maidenhead Mtn., but government surveyors changed the name in the 1920s. Inexplicably, they did not change the name of the nearby creek, Maidenhead Branch, which still appears on modern maps. Hellgate Ridge is the only other example of this category in the Pedlar District.

The origin of the name of Mt. Pleasant is uncertain. It may be named for the Pleasants family of Amherst County, but local reports claim that it is of greater antiquity. Its appearance on the Fry-Jefferson map of 1751 tends to confirm this. Also, the prefix "Mt." tends to cast doubt on its being a derivation from a personal name. Most likely, it is a descriptive name.

Another mystery is raised by Torry Mtn. and Torry Ridge. A search of records has revealed no such family name. "Torry" is perhaps a corruption of "Tory," and may indicate that this area was populated by tories during the American Revolution.

Enchanted Creek was once corrupted to "Shanty Creek," but the origin of the original name is unknown. Another unsolved question is whether Bee Mtn. is a personal name or a descriptive name. Nothing is known about the origin of the following interesting names: Elephant Mtn., Punchbowl Mtn., Cellar Mtn., Skulking Branch, Dancing Creek, and Love Lady Creek.

The origins of the names of the "religious" mountains is an old and popular controversy. The Priest appears on the Fry-Jefferson map of 1751 as "Priest Mtn." Robert Rose's diary mentions "Priest's Mtn." in a 1749 entry. Dr. Ruskin S. Freer, in the *Lynchburg News* for March 26, 1950, reported that a Du Priest family were early settlers in the Tye River valley. No doubt remains that The Priest was owned by Du Priest and was the first of the "religious" mountains to be named. "Bald Friar" also appears on the Fry-Jefferson map. It seems likely that this was an imaginative invention that was suggested by the name "Priest's Mtn."

Although the foregoing discredits two alternative theories, these theories might be correct as an explanation for the origin of The Cardinal. Shortly before the Civil War, some Polish-Catholic immigrants settled briefly on the headwaters of Piney River. They attempted to turn the mountainside (probably of The Cardinal) into a vineyard, but the enterprise failed. It is a strong possibility that this group, influenced by the existence of The Priest and The Friar, named their mountain "The Cardinal."

The second theory is based on a legend reported by Dr. Freer and confirmed by Parkway Ranger Bill Lord. According to Dr. Freer, W.E. Massie of Tyro says that local legend maintains that a monastery had once been located in the "religious" mountains, and that someone had once discovered the foundations of the monastery's building. If this is true, it is another possible source for the origin of The Cardinal; but Alfred Percy casts doubt on this theory by suggesting that the legendary monastery is a confusion of the actual Polish-Catholic community.

I have saved the most important result of my research until last. While scouting the trails in this book, I noticed that several local residents referred to Cole Mtn. as "Cold Mtn." At first this seemed like merely a corruption due to the similarity of the names. Later, during my research on early, local surnames, I found that while "Coleman" is common, "Cole" never appears in the records. I began to wonder whether "Cole" was the corrupted form. Then I discovered that Alfred Percy refers to "Cold Mtn." on pages six and seven of his book, *Old Place Names* (referenced above). There was no doubt that Mr. Percy was referring to Cole Mtn., but the possibility remained that he was merely passing on a local corruption. While searching through land grant records, I found the indisputable answer to the question. On April 10, 1781, Samuel Higginbotham was granted 140 acres on the side of "Cold Mountain" and the south branches of Buffalo River. The reference to Buffalo River removes any doubt that this might apply to some mountain other than Cole Mtn. Furthermore, "Cold Mtn." makes a great deal of sense as a descriptive name. Being completely bald, and having an elevation of 4,022 feet, this mountain is probably exceptionally cold in windy weather. The corruption from "Cold" to "Cole" probably occurred when the U.S.G.S. first began work on comprehensive topographic maps of the United States. The error is already present on the oldest map of the area in my possession, a 1936 Forest Service map of George Washington National Forest.

Green Pond

Indian Rocks

Geology of the Pedlar District

During the late Pre-Cambrian and Cambrian eras (800 to 600 million years ago), the area of the Appalachian range was the site of considerable volcanic activity. At least seven distinct lava flows deposited layers of igneous rock, most of it later metamorphosing to granite and gneiss. The accumulated thickness of this rock was about 1,500 feet.

At the start of the Paleozoic era (600 million years ago), most of the east coast of North America, including the Appalachian area, was covered with large inland seas. Sedimentary layers of clay, sand, and mud filled with lime were deposited. Over a long period of time, the vertical pressure converted these into shale, sandstone, and limestone respectively.

The lateral pressure created by colliding continental plates caused the uplift of the Appalachian mountains during the late Paleozoic era (about 250 million years ago). In many spots, the once horizontal layers of sedimentary rock were tilted vertically, thus exposing softer rock which then began to erode. The folding, fracturing, and erosion of the crust involved in the uplift resulted in a series of generally parallel ridges. At the same time, the pressures that caused the uplift also changed the nature of many of the rocks. Basalt and sandstone were changed into greenstone and quartz respectively; and more rarely, shale was transformed into slate.

The first uplift exposed what is known as the Summit Peneplain, which includes those flattish mountain peaks and ridges that are usually 3,500 feet and higher. Two more uplifts, starting in the late Mesozoic era (Cretaceous period, about 135 million years ago), exposed two more erosion levels, known as the Upland and Intermediate Peneplains. Those broad, rounded peaks in the Blue Ridge, at about 2,400 to 3,000 feet, belong to the Upland Peneplain; and the spur ridges and foothills, at about 2,300 feet and less, belong to the Intermediate Peneplain.

The final uplift occurred during the late Tertiary period of the Cenozoic era (about seven million years ago), and exposed the Valley-floor, or Shenandoah Peneplain. This uplift caused the final draining of an inland sea that had been trapped inside the valley by the Blue Ridge uplift.

The older, base rock in the center of the Blue Ridge acted as a barrier between the predominantly sedimentary rock of the west and the igneous and metamorphic rock of the east. Along the Augusta County-Nelson County border, the following igneous and metamorphic rocks can be found: slate, schist, quartzite, marble, phyllite, conglomerite, greenstone, diorite, and gabbro. Torry Ridge is almost entirely gneiss. From The Priest to the vicinity of US-60, granite and gneiss predominate along the Blue Ridge. The entire area south of US-60 is composed primarily of shale, as well as such sedimentary rocks as limestone, sandstone, and dolomite. Big Levels is composed largely of a type of sandstone known as the Antietam formation, the same kind of rock that composes many of the outlying ridges of Shenandoah National Park's southern section. Fine, straight, parallel tubes that cross the rock's bedding at right angles characterize this stone (sometimes called "pipe-rock" because of its appearance). These tubes are the fossilized burrows (holes filled with sand that later hardened) of an ancient sea-worm, skolithos. The estimated age of these fossilized wormholes is half a billion years.

Extensive mining of iron and manganese occurred in many areas of the Pedlar District during the nineteenth century. Tin was also mined in the Irish Creek valley for a long time. Zinc and lead deposits can be found in the sedimentary rock areas, but they are not large enough for commercial mining.

Several semiprecious and ornamental stones can be found in or near the Pedlar District. Deposits of amethyst are north of Lowesville and in the Irish Creek valley. Also found in the Irish Creek valley are zircon, tourmaline, beryl, fluorite, apatite, moonstone, and labradorite. Deposits of moonstone and labradorite occur near Montebello, too. Along the Appalachian Trail, unakite can be found as far south as the Tye River Gap. A famous unakite location is in a cliff beside Va-56, about two miles west of Tye River Gap.

Saint Marys River Falls

Tree on AT near Spy Rock

Flora and Fauna of the Pedlar District

Chestnut oaks, northern red oaks, and red maples are the most common trees in the Pedlar District. Black oak, white oak, scarlet oak, post oak, blackjack oak (rare), striped maple, and sugar maple are also found. Four varieties of pine can be seen: Virginia pine, white pine, pitch pine, and table-mountain pine. Hickory seems to be less common than in Shenandoah National Park. Black tupelo (blackgum) predominates on Big Levels. Notable stands of shagbark hickory are on Tarjacket Ridge, along Little Cove Creek, and near the top of Belle Cove Trail. Hemlocks, yellow birch, and river birch are profuse in wet areas. Catawba rhododendron is abundant throughout the district. American elm and sumac are also common. More rarely, one can find ash, American basswood, common hoptree, American beech, sycamore, and red cedar. Young American chestnut is particularly abundant in the Big Levels area, and some of these exceed ten feet in height.

Wild geraniums and bindweed (a member of the morning glory family) appear to be the most common flowers in spring and early summer. Cardinal flowers, found in wet places, are predominant in late summer. Also found are columbines, asters, evening primroses, black-eyed susans, appendaged waterleaf, smooth false foxglove, and a large variety of ferns. Blueberries are most profuse in the Big Levels area, and strawberries can be found on the slopes of Cole (Cold) Mtn. Kudzu lines many roads in the Pedlar District vicinity, most notably along US-60 between Oronoco and the Blue Ridge Parkway. Poison ivy is relatively rare in the Pedlar District.

Wolves, buffalo, elk, lynx, chamois, roe, and mink once roamed the Blue Ridge mountains and Shenandoah valley. They vanished from the area shortly after the coming of the settlers. The settlers introduced crows, blackbirds, and honeybees to the area.

Today, raccoons, opossums, skunks, woodchucks, grouse, wild turkeys, and other small game are common in the Forest. Deer are rarely seen because the hunting season reduces their population and makes them wary of humans. Bears are virtually non-existent in the Pedlar District, except in the Three Ridges-Meadow Mtn. area. A vast variety of butterflies makes this district ideal for collectors.

In June 1988, I made a rare sighting of two river otters along an upper tributary of the Pedlar River. Even more remarkable was that they were both white (white river otters are especially scarce).

As part of a wildlife preservation program, some peregrine falcons, a rare and endangered species, were released from a blind on Cole (Cold) Mtn. in spring of 1988. They now nest on a nearby mountain.

Three varieties of snakes predominate. The black snake is the most common. Although the black snake is not poisonous, many in the Pedlar District are five to seven feet long and their bite would be quite painful. The poisonous timber rattlesnake is also fairly common. They usually do not move when humans approach. Do not depend on getting a warning from their rattles. Copperheads are rarely seen because they avoid humans. During the scouting of the trails in this book, in the summer of 1980, I saw six black snakes, one rattlesnake, and no copperheads. From other hikers, I received many reports of rattlesnakes and two reports of copperheads. In 1988–89, I saw one rattlesnake and one black snake.

Hunting and fishing are allowed on National Forest land, but state licenses are required, as well as a National Forest Permit (stamp). The season for small game starts around the beginning of October. Deer and bear seasons are usually from mid-November through December. Dates, regulations and fees are variable. Contact the Pedlar Ranger District Headquarters, U.S. Forest Service, 2424 Magnolia Avenue, Buena Vista, VA 24416.

Trail Descriptions

FDR-162

9.9 m.　　　　　　　　　　　　　　　　**PATC map #12: F-7**

This dirt road traverses Big Levels, a plateau over 3,000 feet high. It is essential to any circuit hikes in the area. Only vehicles with high clearance should drive on it. A remnant of the Summit Peneplain, dating before the Blue Ridge upthrust, Big Levels is covered with dense scrub brush, mountain laurel, azalea, Virginia pine, post oak, chestnut oak, and the Pedlar District's most extensive growth of young American chestnuts. The plateau turns fiery red in September due to the abundant black tupelo (blackgum). Good campsites are rare.

Access:

Park at the Bald Mtn. overlook, on the Blue Ridge Parkway between Va-56 and I-64. The southeastern end of the road is next to the overlook.

To reach the northwestern end, from I-64, take US-340 west. Turn left onto Va-608 at Stuart's Draft. Bear left onto Va-610 at fork. Turn right onto Va-660. Pass Shenandoah Acres campground. Va-660 becomes FDR-52 at the Forest boundary. The gate here is closed from January 1 through March 31. Turn right onto FDR-42. The road is on the left and is marked by a sign. There is room for two cars to park here.

Detailed trail data:

0–9.9 Gate beside Bald Mtn. overlook. Ascend.

.7–9.2 Bald Mtn. Trail intersects on left. Level ahead, then descend.

1.0–8.9 Road intersects on right. This road leads to the trailhead for Torry Ridge Trail and to a Forest Service lookout tower in a clearing. This clearing was used by Indians for a signal station in early colonial days. Bear left.

1.3–8.6 Mills Creek Trail intersects on right. Good campsite here.

1.4–8.5 Level. Ahead, short descents alternate with level stretches.

1.9–8.0 Descend steeply.

2.5–7.4 Ascend.

2.9–7.0 Top of Flint Mtn., elevation 3,440 feet. Descend steeply. Lots of large rhododendron and mountain laurel.

3.6–6.3 Ascend generally with some level stretches.

3.8–6.1 Look back for view of Flint Mtn.

4.1–5.8 Junction with Saint Marys River Trail, on the left, and Kennedy Ridge Trail, on the right. Descend ahead, then level.

4.2–5.7 Ascend steeply.

4.3–5.6 Level.

5.4–4.5 Junction with FDR-162A, on left. Go right at fork.

5.5–4.4 Ascend.

5.7–4.2 Descend.

5.9–4.0 Spring on left is the source for Johns Run. Water from this untested source should be boiled before use.

6.0–3.9 Ascend.

6.3–3.6 Descend.

6.4–3.4 Go right at fork. Just ahead are views of the nameless ridge beyond Johns Run.

6.5–3.4 Level. Old road intersects on left. Go straight.

6.6–3.3 Old road intersects on right. Go straight.

6.7–3.2 Descend.

6.9–3.0 Go right at fork. Several good views of the Shenandoah Valley in the next 3 m.

9.8–.1 Go right at fork.

9.9–0 Junction with FDR-42. Distance from here to Kennedy Ridge Trail parking area is 3.0 m.

FDR-162A

1.7 m.   **PATC map #12: F-4**

This link between FDR-162 and Cellar Mtn. Trail follows the route of the former Forest Service Road 162.

Access:

The eastern end is on FDR-162 (see description). The western end joins with the eastern (upper) end of Cellar Mtn. Trail (see description).

Detailed trail data:

0–1.7 Junction with FDR-162. Ascend ahead and pass many large ant mounds.

    .6–1.1 Level, then descend.

    .8–.9 Small pond on left. Ascend.

    .9–.8 Bear left at fork. Pass old timber cut.

1.0–.7 Descend through more usual forest. Less scrub growth and wetter, better soil.

1.5–.2 Ascend back into scrub growth.

1.7–0 Junction with Cellar Mtn. Trail, on left at fork. FDR-162A continues to right and soon dead-ends near a knoll.

BALD MOUNTAIN TRAIL

2.2 m   **PATC map #12: G-7**

This yellow-blazed trail, constructed and maintained by the Forest Service, is one of the more beautiful trails in the Pedlar District. Part of the Saint Marys Wilderness Area (see "Hiking in the Pedlar District"), it can be hiked on an excellent 10.7 m. circuit with Mine Bank Trail, Saint Marys River Trail, and FDR-162.

Access:

The eastern end is on FDR-162 (see description).
The western end is on Mine Bank Trail (see description).

Detailed trail data:

0–2.2   Junction on FDR-162. Trail is not marked by sign. Look for yellow blaze. Descend through northern red oak, red maple, chestnut oak, American chestnut shoots, and lots of mountain laurel.

.5–1.7   Descend into deep ravine.

.6–1.6   Cross intermittent creek in dark hemlock grove. Extremely treacherous footing. Ahead, cross creek again. Lots of yellow birch.

.7–1.5   Cross creek again.

.9–1.3   Lots of large rhododendron and river birch. Level.

1.0–1.2   Ascend with good footing on old road. Lots of grass, moss, and ferns.

1.9–.3   Go right at fork.

2.2–0   Intersect Mine Bank Trail about 140 yards from the Blue Ridge Parkway, on the left.

MINE BANK TRAIL

2.1 m   **PATC map #12: E-7**

This orange-blazed trail, constructed and maintained by the Forest Service, is one of the most scenic trails in the Pedlar District. It descends the narrow canyon of Mine Bank Creek and features dark hemlock groves and impressive cliffs. The footing is dangerous in some places, so caution should be exercised, especially in wet or icy weather. Part of the Saint Marys Wilderness Area (see "Hiking in the Pedlar District"), this trail can be hiked on an excellent 10.7 m. circuit with Saint Marys River Trail, FDR-162, and Bald Mtn. Trail.

Access:

Park at the Fork Mtn. overlook on the Blue Ridge Parkway between I-64 and Va-56. The trailhead is a gravel road on the opposite side of the Parkway about 50 yards south of the overlook.

The northern end of this trail intersects the Saint Marys River Trail (see description).

Detailed trail data:

0–2.1   Blue Ridge Parkway. Gravel road soon becomes dirt. In 70 yards, go straight onto footpath where road bears left.

.1–2.0 Bald Mtn. Trail, blazed yellow and marked by sign, intersects on right. Bear left and descend.

.2–1.9 Descend very steeply just ahead, through sassafras, white oak, maple, young chestnut, laurel, and azalea.

.5–1.6 Descend gently near stream.

.7–1.4 Lots of hemlock and large rhododendron.

.8–1.3 Canyon becomes deep and dark. Yellow birch and lady fern.

.9–1.2 Cross creek.

1.0–1.1 Cross creek, then look back at the interesting sedimentary strata of the creek bedrock.

1.1–1.0 Cross creek.

1.2–.9 Cross creek. Just ahead, cross a branch of the creek.

1.3–.8 Impressive cliffs on left.

1.4–.7 The canyon becomes very narrow, and the footing becomes rocky and hazardous. Many interesting rock formations.

1.6–.5 The canyon opens up. Large rhododendron just ahead.

1.9–.2 Descend gently in Saint Marys River valley. Mountain laurel.

2.0–.1 Level.

2.1–0 Intersect Saint Marys River Trail. FDR-162 is 3.0 m. to right; trailhead is 3.6 m. to left.

SAINT MARYS RIVER TRAIL

6.6 m. **PATC map #12: C-5**

This blue-blazed trail, part of the Saint Marys Wilderness Area (see "Hiking in the Pedlar District"), contains a variety of features that make it one of the most interesting in the Pedlar District. Views of the river and surrounding cliffs, cascades, and the remains of two mines are among the attractions. An abundant growth of blueberries may be found along the trail and especially on Big Levels, at the trail's terminus. A spur trail, described separately below, leads to a waterfall.

Access:

From I-64, take US-340 west. Turn left onto Va-608 at Stuart's Draft. Follow Va-608 signs for about 12.5 miles. After passing Mt. Joy

Presbyterian Church on right, turn left onto FDR-41. Drive to end of road, where there is ample parking.

From I-81, take US-11 to Va-666. From Va-666, turn right onto Va-608, then see above.

The eastern end of this trail intersects FDR-162 at 4.1 miles from Blue Ridge Parkway.

Detailed trail data:

0–6.6 Rock at end of parking lot. Go left at fork. Campsites along the river, and swimming, are possible near the beginning of the trail. Ahead, the trail alternately follows or parallels a rocky, intermittent stream, probably an eroded road, or the bed of the old railroad that once ran up this hollow.

.6–6.0 Untested spring on left. Water should be boiled before use.

1.0–5.6 Cross very rocky delta. This is a flood-plain. Lots of sumac and sweet birch.

1.2–5.4 Go right at fork and cross Saint Marys River just ahead. This crossing will be difficult or impossible in high water.

1.3–5.3 View of Cellar Mtn. cliffs on left. Trail follows narrow, eroded ledge by river, so exercise great caution.

1.4–5.2 Good campsite. Straight ahead, a spur trail leads .8 m. to a waterfall (see separate entry below). The Saint Marys River Trail turns right and ascends with Sugartree Branch on left. Some hemlocks are here.

1.6–5.0 A cliff rises from the trail on the right.

1.7–4.9 Small waterfall (5–10 feet) and pool. Lots of river birch.

1.8–4.8 Cross clearing, then turn left and cross creek.

2.1–4.5 Go right. To left of trail are ruins of a former, manganese-iron, surface-mining operation, now overgrown with Virginia pine. Iron slag litters the trail ahead.

2.2–4.4 Path on right leads a few feet to narrow view of mountains to south. Just ahead, go left at fork. (Right fork leads a few yards to excellent view of deep, surface-mining excavation that looks like a canal.) In 35 yards past left fork, a concrete foundation and some boards are all that remain of an old metal shed. The top of the hill on the left, at this point, provides a fine view of a large earthen reservoir, now dry. Descend ahead along a pleasant grassy trail with good footing.

2.5–4.1 Cross intermittent stream and ascend.

2.7–3.9 Descend.

3.2–3.4 Rhododendron and mountain laurel.

3.3–3.3 Go straight. Old road on right leads to another mine. Just ahead, bear left, cross creek, and ascend.

3.4–3.2 Possible camp on right, at mouth of intersecting old road that leads to mining excavation in a few yards. Lots of slag here. Level just ahead.

3.6–3.0 Mine Bank Trail intersects on right.

3.7–2.9 Cross creek. Trail ascends, descends, and then becomes level.

3.8–2.8 Cross intermittent stream.

3.9–2.7 Cross intermittent stream, then another stream.

4.0–2.6 This is a much older, abandoned, surface-mining operation. Everything is extensively overgrown. Note large mounds of excavated earth. On the right are ruins consisting of iron bolts embedded in concrete, perhaps the base for some heavy machinery. Excellent campsites, under sycamores, are on left. Bear right, around ruins, and ascend ahead, sometimes steeply.

4.4–2.2 Level. Descend ahead.

4.7–1.9 Cross Chimney Branch and ascend.

4.8–1.8 Descend and cross Saint Marys River, now a small stream, just ahead.

5.1–1.5 Cross stream. Lots of rhododendron and mountain laurel. Ahead, begin an ascent of 640 feet over the next mile, which soon becomes very rocky.

6.0–.6 Good view of the river valley.

6.1–.5 Trail becomes generally level. This is the Big Levels plateau, a remnant of the Summit Peneplain, dating before the Blue Ridge upthrust. The plateau is densely overgrown with underbrush, including mountain laurel. Black tupelo (blackgum), pine, post oak, chestnut oak, and sassafras predominate. Big Levels also has the Pedlar District's most extensive growth of young American chestnut.

6.3–.3 Former junction of Forest Service Road 162, now blocked off, is reverting to a grassy clearing, the best campsite on Big Levels. Blueberries can be found in the vicinity. Straight ahead, a path leads to Green Pond in a few yards. Like Big Meadows, in Shenandoah National Park, Green Pond is an undrained portion of the Summit Peneplain. Once a three-acre bog, Green Pond has unfortunately shrunk by about one-third since 1980.

To continue on the trail, follow the old road (formerly Kennedy Ridge Trail) on left of path to pond. In 70 yards, go right at fork. In another 35 yards, go right off road and onto path.

6.6–0 Stile at four-way junction. FDR-162 leads to Cellar Mtn. Trail in 3.1 m. to left, and to Blue Ridge Parkway in 4.1 m. to right. Straight ahead, Kennedy Ridge Trail begins.

SAINT MARYS RIVER WATERFALL TRAIL

Access:

See description for Saint Marys River Trail.

Detailed trail data:

0–.8 Junction with Saint Marys River Trail. Go straight on reddish orange-blazed trail. Cross river in 90 yards and proceed upstream.

.3–.5 Cross intermittent stream. Sassafras, rhododendron, and mountain laurel ahead.

.5–.3 Cliff and rockslides on left. Hemlock.

.6–.2 Pool on right. Interesting overhanging rock. Just ahead, cross river at an angle and climb eroded bank on other side.

.8–0 Clearing beside cliff. Good campsite, but dangerous for children because it sits on a ledge of the cliff. View of waterfall (15–20 feet) is about 50 yards farther.

CELLAR MOUNTAIN TRAIL

3.3 m.   **PATC map #12: F-4**

This blue-blazed trail, constructed and maintained by the Forest Service, is a part of the Saint Marys Wilderness Area (see "Hiking in the Pedlar District"). It offers a superb view of the Shenandoah Valley. The trail data begins at the intersection with FDR-162A, because this trail is most useful for circuit hike in conjunction with Saint Marys River Trail, which has better parking.

Access:

From I-64, take US-340 west. Turn left onto Va-608 at Stuart's Draft. Follow Va-608 signs for about 12.5 miles. After passing Mt. Joy Presbyterian Church on right, turn left onto FDR-41. Turn left onto FDR-42. Sign on right marks trailhead. There is room for two cars to park.

From I-81, take US-11 to Va-666. From Va-666, turn right onto Va-608, then see above.

The eastern end of this trail intersects FDR-162A.

Detailed trail data:

0–3.3 Junction with FDR-162A.

.1–3.2 Go left at fork, off old road and onto path. Descend with good footing ahead, through rhododendron, mountain laurel, oak, and American chestnut shoots.

.3–3.0 Level.

.4–2.9 Ascend steeply.

.6–2.7 Trail is generally level as it follows a ridge. Some mediocre views of Saint Marys River valley and Mine Bank Mtn. are on left. Footing is often rocky along here.

.9–2.4 Descend.

1.1–2.2 Ascend slightly, then more steeply.

1.3–2.0 Level. On right, the peak of Cellar Mtn., at 3,640 feet, is the highest in the Big Levels area.

1.4–1.9 Descend slightly.

1.5–1.8 Ascend slightly.

1.6–1.7 Descend into open forest with possible campsites all along the way. The forest is almost exclusively oak, with northern red oak predominating.

1.8–1.5 View on left.

2.1–1.2 View of Shenandoah Valley on left. Descend through pine, post oak, and extensive scrub.

2.4–.9 Excellent view of Shenandoah Valley all along here. Abundant blueberries.

3.0–.3 Spring on right. Water from this untested source should be boiled before use. A possible campsite is just ahead.

3.3–0 FDR-42. To return to parking area at Saint Marys River Trail, turn left on FDR-42, then left on FDR-41. The distance back is 1.9 m.

KENNEDY RIDGE TRAIL

3.3 m.   **PATC map #12: J-4**

Except for one view from a rock outcrop, this trail has no special feature to commend it. It is useful for circuit hikes.

Access:

From I-64, take US-340 west. Turn left onto Va-608 at Stuart's Draft. Bear left onto Va-610 at fork. Turn right onto Va-660. Pass Shenandoah Acres campground. Va-660 becomes FDR-52 at Forest boundary. The gate here is closed from January 1 through March 31. Turn left onto FDR-42. The trail is the third road on the right, but one must park in the big field at the second road on the right, and then walk the short distance to the trail.

The southern end of this trail intersects FDR-162.

Detailed trail data:

0–3.3 Trailhead on FDR-42. This trail follows a very steep, sunny, rocky, dirt road that is suitable only for vehicles with high clearance. The road is lined almost exclusively with Virginia pine and white pine.

.4–2.9 Possible campsite. Normal deciduous forest begins.

1.8–1.5 Mediocre views on both sides. The road becomes a path and bears left.

1.9–1.4 View of nameless ridge to west from rock outcrop on right. Descend steeply to right.

2.0–1.3 Ascend steeply on narrow path through dense rhododendron and mountain laurel.

2.1–1.2 Trail becomes a road again.

2.4–.9 Good campsite on left.

2.5–.8 Level.

2.7–.6 Ascend, then level.

3.0–.3 Descend steeply.

3.1–.2 Trail levels off. This is the Big Levels plateau, a remnant of the Summit Peneplain, dating before the Blue Ridge upthrust. The plateau is densely overgrown with underbrush, including mountain laurel. Black tupelo (blackgum), pine, post oak, chestnut oak, and sassafras predominate. Big Levels also has the

Pedlar District's most extensive growth of young American chestnuts.

3.3–0 Junction with Saint Marys River Trail, straight ahead, and FDR-162, on left and right.

TORRY RIDGE TRAIL

7.3 m.   **PATC map #12: L-8**

This yellow-blazed trail, constructed and maintained by the Forest Service, is particularly useful for circuit hikes. It is a very rugged trail, however, because of the terribly rocky footing. Also, the trail is often exposed, is extremely hot in summer, and lacks any water source; thus, it is recommended that a large quantity of water be carried. The trail offers some good views of the Back Creek and Mills Creek valleys.

Access:

From I-64, take Va-624 to Lyndhurst. Turn left onto Va-664. Park at Mt. Torry Furnace, on the right. There is room for only a few cars here.

The southwest end of this trail is on the lookout tower access road off FDR-162 (see description).

Detailed trail data:

0–7.3 Mt. Torry Furnace. This was a hot-blast, charcoal furnace used for smelting iron ore. Built in 1804, it was owned during the Civil War by the Tredegar family, the great iron-mongers of the Confederacy. Destroyed by Duffie's Union raiders in June 1864, it was rebuilt in January 1865, and operated until 1884. The trail begins on the left side of the furnace. Ascend through chestnut oak, post oak, blackjack oak, Virginia pine, beech, yellow poplar, sassafras, mountain laurel, and rhododendron.

.1–7.2 Go left at fork.

1.0–6.3 Mills Creek Trail intersects on right. Bear left. Ascend steeply.

1.3–6.0 Good view of Blue Ridge and Back Creek valley. Descend just ahead.

1.4–5.9 Trail ascends to, and descends from, a couple of knolls in the next 1.7 m.

3.1–4.2 Blue Loop Trail (east side) intersects on the left. Bear right.

3.3–4.0 Descend.

3.4–3.9 Ascend to crest, then descend.

3.6–3.7 Level, then ascend.

4.0–3.3 A fine view of Sherando Lake. After crossing the rockpile just ahead, the trail becomes level.

4.2–3.1 Blue Loop Trail (west side) intersects on left. Torry Ridge Spring is a steep .6 m. down the Blue Loop Trail. A mileage sign is here.

4.4–2.9 Ascend.

4.6–2.7 Descend.

4.9–2.4 Ascend steeply. Good views along here of the Mill Creek valley and Kelley Mtn., on the right, and of Upper Lake and the Blue Ridge Parkway, on the left.

5.4–1.9 Descend.

5.6–1.7 Ascend.

6.1–1.2 The Slacks Trail intersects on the left. The mileage sign here says "White Rock Gap Trail 2.2," but does not name The Slacks Trail. The correct distance to the White Rock Gap Trail is 2.6 m. Virginia pine, post oak, mountain laurel, and rhododendron predominate. Ascend generally.

6.5–.8 View of Kelley Mtn. and rockslide on right.

7.0–.3 Descend. Excellent view of Mills Creek valley all along here.

7.1–.2 Ascend.

7.3–0 Intersect the road to the Bald Mtn. lookout tower. The lookout tower is a short distance to the left. The junction with FDR-162 is .1 m. to the right. To reach the Mills Creek Trail, go right on FDR-162 and hike .3 m. to intersection. Total distance between Torry Ridge Trail and Mills Creek Trail is .4 m.

MILLS CREEK TRAIL

6.8 m.   **PATC map #12: G-7**

This blue-blazed trail, constructed and maintained by the Forest Service, has an unusual feature. The forest of the creek valley was "thinned" by the Forest Service in 1973. "Thinning" is a process in which the less desirable trees are cut down to allow more room for the best trees to grow. The result is that this forest, composed almost exclusively of northern red oak and chestnut oak, has a unique, sparse look. This stand of trees will be harvested about 40 years from now. Because of the increase in the amount of sunlight that reaches the ground, dense undergrowth fills the valley. The trail also passes through a former strip-mine.

Access:

The southwest end is on FDR-162 (see description). The northeast end is on Torry Ridge Trail (see description).

Detailed trail data:

0–6.8 Intersection with FDR-162. A good campsite is here. Descend.

.1–6.7 On the left side of the trail, a deep, wide crack in the ground appears to be a cave entrance. This site is not listed in *Caves of Virginia*, however. Any attempt to explore this crack would be extremely dangerous because the shale is very brittle and the earth is usually very dry. Descend steeply with bad footing.

1.0–5.8 Cross tributary of Mills Creek. An untested spring is on the left. Water should be boiled before use. This creekbed is approximately 20 feet wide and five feet deep. When this trail was scouted, however, during a summer drought, both spring and creek were completely dry. The trail parallels the creek and is obscure at times.

1.2–5.6 Cross Mills Creek in wide, flat valley. The "thinned" forest begins here. Ahead, bear left on old road.

1.6–5.2 A pleasant, grassy area on left. This is the best campsite on this trail.

1.8–5.0 Cross stream.

2.4–4.4 Mills Creek on left.

2.5–4.3 The ruins of a bridge have been bulldozed to the right side of the trail. Cross creek just ahead and climb embankment.

2.6–4.2 Old road intersects on right. Go straight.

2.8–4.0 Trail has eroded and fallen into creek. Go down steep embankment.

3.2–3.6 Ruins of bridge. Cross creek just ahead.

3.3–3.5 Ruins of bridge. Cross creek.

3.4–3.4 Small cliff on left. Trail undulates ahead.

3.9–2.9 Leave "thinned" forest. Normal forest growth begins.

4.0–2.8 Turn right at clearing. Cross creek and go up hill. Trail to left leads down to a lake (no fishing allowed).

4.1–2.7 Large grassy clearing. This was formerly a strip-mine.

4.6–2.2 Old trail intersects on left. Go straight.

4.9–1.9 Bear left.

5.0–1.8 Pass gate.

5.2–1.6 Good campsite on right.

5.4–1.4 Cross creek at bend in road. Ascend and go left at fork ahead.

5.5–1.3 Go straight through cross-road. An old timber cut is on the right.

5.6–1.2 Bear left and descend short distance to a level pine needle trail.

6.0–.8 Go right at fork.

6.1–.7 Cross creek, turn right, and ascend steeply through mountain laurel.

6.4–.4 View of Waynesboro on left. The trail becomes very rocky here.

6.8–0 Intersect Torry Ridge Trail. Trail to left leads to Mt. Torry Furnace. Trail to right leads over ridge.

THE SLACKS TRAIL

2.6 m.   **PATC map #12: G-8**

This blue-blazed trail, constructed and maintained by the Forest Service, has no distinctive features, but it is very useful for circuit hikes. The trail description is presented in two sections based upon the most common direction of travel.

Access:

The northern end of this trail intersects Torry Ridge Trail, and the southern end intersects White Rock Gap Trail. The easiest access is from The Slacks overlook, which is on the Blue Ridge Parkway between I-64 and Va-56. Follow the trail from the picnic table 90 yards to a trail crossing. Turn left and go 130 more yards to the junction with The Slacks Trail. Turn left for the northern section, or turn right for the southern section.

Detailed trail data (northern section):

0–.8 Junction with access trail from overlook. Red maple, chestnut oak, hickory, sassafras. Descend.

.1–.7 Ascend. Another access trail from the overlook intersects on the left. Good views of the opposite ridge and the valley below (which holds a tributary of Back Creek) are all along this ridge. The footing becomes very rocky, and several small rockslides must be crossed.

.8–0 Good long view of the Sherando Lake area. Ahead, intersect Torry Ridge Trail. A mileage sign here says "White Rock Gap Trail 2.2," but does not name The Slacks Trail. The correct distance to White Rock Gap Trail is 2.6 m.

Detailed trail data (southern section):

0–1.8 Junction with access trail from overlook. Ascend through red maple, chestnut oak, and hickory.

.1–1.7 Trail undulates gently. Sassafras, mountain laurel, and American chestnut sprouts.

.3–1.5 Ascend.

.4–1.4 Reach top of ridge and descend.

.7–1.1 View of Torry Ridge on left.

.9–.9 Good view of Torry Ridge on left.

1.0–.8 Cross intermittent stream and ascend slightly.

1.3–.5 Descend. Lots of daisy-family flowers.

1.4–.4 Descend very steeply.

1.5–.3 Old road intersects on right. Bear left.

1.7–.1 Good view of ridge on right.

1.8–0 Intersect White Rock Gap Trail. A mileage sign here says "Torry Ridge Trail 2.2," but does not name The Slacks Trail. The correct distance is 2.6 m.

WHITE ROCK FALLS TRAIL

2.5 m.   **PATC map #12: G-9**

This yellow-blazed trail, constructed by the Youth Conservation Corps in 1979, is maintained by the Tidewater Appalachian Trail Club. The trail's highlight is a most impressive gorge, which has a waterfall and natural wading pool. The trail can be hiked on an excellent 4.7 m. circuit with portions of The Slacks Trail and the White

Rock Gap Trail. The name "White Rock" derives from the abundant quartz found in the area.

Access:

Park at The Slacks overlook on the Blue Ridge Parkway between I-64 and Va-56. Hike the southern section of The Slacks Trail (see description) to White Rock Gap Trail (see description). Turn right and follow White Rock Gap Trail to its end on the Blue Ridge Parkway. Cross parkway to trailhead on other side. Another possibility is to park at Sherando Lake (see description) and follow the entire length of the White Rock Gap Trail.

The northern end of the trail is on the Blue Ridge Parkway about 60 yards north of The Slacks overlook. It is marked by a sign that is difficult to see from the parkway.

Detailed trail data:

0–2.5 Trailhead opposite White Rock Gap Trail. An old road, now blocked off, descends to the left of the trail. Ahead, descend through post oak, hickory, white pine, yellow poplar, and chestnut oak.

.3–2.2 Grassy area with old wall along stream on left. The hollow to left has many large boulders with remarkable, flat faces.

.4–2.1 View of creek. American basswood is abundant here.

.5–2.0 Old road intersects on left.

.7–1.8 Go right at fork, off road and onto path. Ascend slightly through mountain laurel and white pine. Ahead, trail undulates while generally descending. Good, broad, winter view of surrounding mountains ahead.

1.2–1.3 Easy creek crossing over many large boulders. A few hemlocks are here. (Note: in opposite direction, left turn across creek is easy to miss.) Ascend along creek.

1.3–1.2 Switchback to left, the first in a series of four, and ascend steeply. View of cliffs from next switchback.

1.4–1.1 Old route intersects on right. Ascend very steeply.

1.5–1.0 Switchback.

1.6–.9 Cliffs overhang the trail here. Turn left. The path to the right leads 100 yards along the cliff to a dark, round gorge with impressive overhanging cliffs. White Rock Falls, a narrow waterfall, is here. This exceptionally beautiful spot also has a wading pool, but one must be careful of slippery rocks and the possibility of snakes.

1.7–.8   Ascend briefly, then descend.

1.9–.6   Top of cliff. Great view from rocks on right.

2.0–.5   Cross intermittent stream, ascend briefly, and then descend through lots of rhododendron, mountain laurel, and hemlock.

2.1–.4   Turn right and cross creek. A large hemlock straight ahead signals this turn, which might otherwise be missed. Good campsite in clearing under hemlocks straight ahead.

2.3–.2   Cross creek on bridge. Virgin hemlock on right after crossing. Ascend.

2.5–0   Blue Ridge Parkway. The Slacks overlook is 60 yards to left.

SHERANDO LAKE ACCESS

From I-64, take Va-624 to Lyndhurst. Turn left onto Va-664. Follow Va-664 to FDR-91, on the right. This is marked with a sign for the Sherando Lake Recreation Area.

From Va-56, go north on the Blue Ridge Parkway. Turn left onto Va-814. Turn left onto FDR-91.

WHITE ROCK GAP TRAIL

2.7 m.   **PATC map #12: I-8**

This orange-blazed trail, constructed and maintained by the Forest Service, follows the course of Back Creek to its headwater. An old cabin site is passed along the way. The name "White Rock" derives from the abundant quartz found in the area.

Access:

See description for Sherando Lake Access. Park in the last lot, next to campground "B." Follow FDR-91 to the trailhead, on the left, near the end of the road.

The western end of the trail is on the Blue Ridge Parkway, opposite White Rock Falls Trail, about .7 m. south of The Priest overlook.

Detailed trail data:

0–2.7   Red gate. Cross open field with Upper Lake on the left.

.1–2.6   Bear right off road and onto path up hill. Good view of Upper Lake. Good footing. The trail soon becomes level. Red maple, post oak, and sassafras.

.4–2.3   Cross intermittent stream. Ascend.

.6–2.1   Possible campsite on the creek flats on the left. Lots of lady fern and common bracken. Level just ahead.

.7–2.0   Turn right at junction.

.9–1.8   Go left at fork, cross intermittent stream and ascend ahead.

1.2–1.5   Descend, cross intermittent stream, and ascend.

2.1–.6   Cross creek.

2.3–.4   The Slacks Trail intersects on the right. A mileage sign here says "Torry Ridge Trail 2.2," but does not name The Slacks Trail. The correct distance is 2.6 m. Bear left and ascend through hemlock, white pine, yellow poplar, and common hoptree.

2.4–.3   Former cabin site and farm are marked by a Forest Service sign. No visible ruins; only typically dense undergrowth. Honeylocust and mountain maple. Ahead, a Forest Service sign marks the headwater of the north fork of Back Creek. This is the watershed for Sherando Lake.

2.7–0   End on Blue Ridge Parkway, opposite the trailhead for White Rock Falls Trail.

UPPER LAKE TRAIL

1.0 m.   **PATC map # 12: I-8**

This unblazed trail, shown only on the inset of PATC map #12, circles Upper Lake and offers some good views up and down the valley.

Access:

See description for Sherando Lake Access and White Rock Gap Trail.

Detailed trail data:

0–1.0   Bear left toward the earthen dam from the trailhead of White Rock Gap Trail.

.1–.9 Ascend earthen dam. The top of the dam offers good views up and down the Back Creek valley.

.3–.7 Turn right at intersection and descend. The trail now undulates as it parallels the lake shore. Chestnut oak, northern red oak, red maple, and hickory.

.5–.5 Cross intermittent creek, then cross footbridge over stream. Sycamore and hemlock are just ahead.

.6–.4 Turn right at junction with old road.

.8–.2 Turn right onto path, cross bridge, and then turn left.

.9–.1 End of loop around lake. Bear left across open field.

1.0–0 End of trailhead for White Rock Gap Trail.

STONY HILL LOOP TRAIL

.2 m.   **PATC map # 12: I-8**

This is a nature trail constructed by the Youth Conservation Corps in 1976–77.

Access:

See description for Sherando Lake Access. Park in the last lot, next to campground "B." The trail is across the road a short distance away.

BLUE LOOP TRAIL

3.7 m.   **PATC map #12: J-8**

This blue-blazed trail, constructed and maintained by the Forest Service, provides access to Torry Ridge from the Sherando Lake area and offers some good views. Because part of this trail duplicates Torry Ridge Trail, and another part follows FDR-91, only the two sections that connect the valley with Torry Ridge are described here.

Access:

See description for Sherando Lake Access. Park in lot on right, next to the fishing regulations sign.

Detailed trail data (eastern side):

0–.8 The trail is level at the beginning, but soon becomes extremely steep. The footing is very slippery because of loose rock. Sassafras, black oak, and mountain laurel predominate.

.3–.5 Excellent view of valley and rockslides on Torry Ridge. The trail is less steep from here on.

.8–0 Junction with Torry Ridge Trail. Turn left and hike 1.1 m. to reach the intersection with the western side of Blue Loop Trail.

Detailed trail data (western side):

0–.8 Mileage sign at junction with Torry Ridge Trail. Descend.

.2–.6 Excellent view of Sherando Lake from Lookout Rock. The descent from here is very steep with horrible footing over rockslides.

.6–.2 Torry Ridge Spring. Water from this untested source should be boiled before use. It had water when scouted during a severe drought.

.7–.1 Turn left at water tank.

.8–0 Campground "A," near the administration building. Follow FDR-91 1.0 m. back to beginning of loop.

LAKESIDE TRAIL

1.2 m.   **PATC map #12: J-8**

This easy, unblazed trail circles Sherando Lake.

Access:

See description for Sherando Lake Access. Park at lot beside Sherando Lake.

Detailed trail data:

0–1.2 Parking lot. Cross footbridge, turn left at bath-house, then right at kiosk. Just ahead, on the right, a mileage sign marks the intersection with the Cliff Trail.

.2–1.0 Go up and down small hill, then the trail is generally level.

.5–.7 Cliff trail intersects on right. Turn left and cross earthen dam to causeway. Descend beside causeway to creek.

.6–.6	Cross creek and ascend.
.7–.5	Path on right leads to rockslide. Bear left.
.8–.4	Trail intersects on right. Bear left.
.9–.3	Bridge over ravine. Descend just ahead.
1.0–.2	Trail intersects on right. Bear left.
1.1–.1	Trail intersects on right. Bear left.
1.2–0	End of loop.

CLIFF TRAIL

.8 m.   PATC map #12: J-8

Access:

See descriptions for Sherando Lake Access and Lakeside Trail.

Detailed trail data:

0–.8   Intersection with Lakeside Trail, in back of bathhouse. Mileage sign. Ascend.

.1–.7   Path intersects on left. Go straight, then bear left off old road.

.5–.3   Lots of mountain laurel and some American chestnut shoots.

.7–.1   Good view of rockslide on Torry Ridge. Descend through sassafras, beech, chestnut oak, and Virginia pine.

.8–0   Intersect Lakeside Trail.

MAU-HAR TRAIL

3.3 m.   PATC map #12: I-11

This blue-blazed trail, constructed in 1979 by the Tidewater Appalachian Trail Club and maintained by that club, is one of the most beautiful trails in the Pedlar District. It provides an excellent circuit hike in conjunction with the AT. Numerous deep pools and a 50-foot waterfall are the highlights of the narrow canyon of Campbell Creek. Along the canyon, the trail is steep and very treacherous. The name derives from the conjunction of Maupin Field Shelter and Harper's Creek.

Access:

Park at Reed's Gap, which is on the Blue Ridge Parkway between I-64 and Va-56. Hike the AT south for 1.8 m. to Maupin Field Shelter.

To reach the southern end, park where the AT crosses Va-56. Hike the AT north for approximately 1.5 m. to intersection with trail, marked by a sign.

Detailed trail data:

0–3.3   Mileage sign beside shelter. Cross creek.

.2–3.1   Descend.

.5–2.8   Cross stream.

.6–2.7   Cross stream over log bridge. Level. Ahead, an untested spring is on the right. Water should be boiled before use.

.7–2.6   Descend steeply, then level.

.9–2.4   Cross creek over log bridge. Ascend through hemlock ahead.

1.0–2.3   Descend.

1.1–2.2   Cross creek over log bridge, and pass through dense rhododendron. Descend very steeply ahead.

1.2–2.1   Scramble over rocks in an impressive gorge. The trail becomes very rocky and treacherous.

1.7–1.6   Excellent view of 50-foot waterfall and deep pool below. Ascend to left, away from the creek.

2.5–.8   Descend to AT.

3.3–0   Junction with AT. Va-56 is about 1.5 m. to the right. Harper's Creek Shelter is about .75 m. to the left. Maupin Field Shelter is about 6.75 m. to the left.

CRABTREE FALLS TRAIL

2.9 m.   **PATC map #12: D-11 or #13: I-3**

This blue-blazed trail has been developed by the Forest Service into a showpiece for the Pedlar District. Bought by the federal government in 1968, the area was made more accessible to the general public by the addition of a gravelled path, stairs over rocks, and railed overlooks. The reason for this attention is that the "grand cataract," with a drop of 500 feet, is the highest waterfall east of the Mississippi River. In addition, the five cascades of Crabtree Falls

Crabtree Falls, the Grand Cataract

have a combined drop of 1,080 feet over a horizontal distance of only 1,800 feet. The falls were probably discovered and named by William Crabtree, a noted colonial backwoodsman and explorer, who settled on the Holston River in 1777. A sawmill once stood along the upper reaches of Crabtree Creek. Crabtree Falls was mentioned several times on the popular television show, "The Waltons."

Camping is prohibited between the creek and trail and within 100 feet on both sides of them.

Access:

The lower end is on Va-56, east of the Blue Ridge Parkway. A large parking area and pit-toilets are here. Night vandalism of cars, especially in winter, is a problem.

The upper end can be reached by taking Va-826, from Va-56, to Crabtree Meadows. Va-826 is a good dirt road that is drivable by cars with two-wheel drive provided they have good clearance beneath them. Crabtree Meadows has a large parking area and pit-toilets.

Detailed trail data:

0–2.9 Parking lot. Cross wooden bridge. Just ahead, a well and pump are on the right, but the water must be boiled before use. A pay-phone is beside the pump. Ascend.

.2–2.7 Overlook with view of cascades. The canyon begins here. Hemlock, yellow birch, striped maple, American elm, and oak predominate along the trail.

.4–2.5 Overlook with a good long view up the canyon and down the precipitous drop. Just ahead is the most vertical of the falls. Lots of spray.

.8–2.1 Overlook with view of cascades and Fork Mtn. Ahead, on the right side of the trail, it is possible to walk through a passageway beneath a pile of boulders.

.9–2.0 A long cascade, down a nearly flat rock face, funnels through some narrows to a pool below.

1.2–1.7 Numerous small cascades over boulders. An extraordinary, colossal hemlock is beside the trail.

1.5–1.4 View from below of the uppermost falls, a long cascade down a large rock face.

1.7–1.2 Top of uppermost falls. Viewpoint to left of trail.

1.8–1.1 Go right at fork.

1.9–1.0 The path is lined with rhododendron and mountain laurel.

2.0–.9 Pass under virgin hemlock grove.

2.1–.8 Old road intersects on left. Just ahead, go right at fork.

2.9–0 Crabtree Meadows. AT is on other side of parking lot. Good campsites are here in the open fields of this gap between The Priest and Maintop Mtn.

FISH HATCHERY TRAIL

1.2 m.   **PATC map #12: A-10 or #13: G-5**

This blue-blazed dirt road offers the easiest access to Spy Rock, one of the most spectacular features of the Pedlar District.

Access:

From Va-56, take Va-690 to the state fish hatchery. This road is unmarked, except for a Virginia Commission of Game and Inland Fisheries sign. Parking is allowed, if permission is asked, from 8:00 a.m. until 4:00 p.m.

The southern end of this trail is on the AT.

Detailed trail data:

0–1.2 Fish hatchery. Ascend with rocky footing through dark hemlocks on blazed dirt road.

.3–.9 Cross intermittent stream.

.7–.5 No more hemlock. Striped maple is predominant.

.8–.4 Go straight up hill at cross-road.

1.2–0 Junction with AT. To reach Spy Rock, go left on AT and ascend. It is .4 m. to Spy Rock from here.

SPY ROCK TRAIL

.1 m.   **PATC map #12: A-11 or #13: H-5**

Spy Rock, at 3,980 feet, offers a 360-degree panoramic view. Next to Cole Mtn. (Cold Mtn.), this is the best view in the Pedlar District. A sign on the AT marks the trailhead. There are many good campsites here. The footpath ends at a curving rock wall that presents a moderately difficult scramble. The rounded top of Spy Rock is gnarly, much eroded, and barren.

Access:

This is accessible only from the AT. The easiest way to reach it is to take the Fish Hatchery Trail (see description) to the AT, and then follow the AT north for .4 m. to the trailhead.

RAILROAD TRAIL (FDR-246)

6.5 m.   **PATC map #13: F-6**

This unblazed, unmaintained old road is useful for circuit hikes in conjunction with the AT. The first third of the trail follows a former railroad bed. Owned by the Southern Lumber Company, the 18 mile railroad was used for hauling lumber, and ore from the Irish Creek tin mine. The railroad was in operation before 1920, and the tracks were still indicated on the 1948 edition of PATC map #12. Blackberry along the trail and saplings more than ten feet high make the trail less exposed and more appealing than ten years ago. Young maples now cover the timber cuts.

Access:

Park at Stillhouse Hollow, which is on the Blue Ridge Parkway between US-60 and Va-56. Hike .3 m. south on the Blue Ridge Parkway to an unpaved road that intersects on the left. This is really the upper portion of Va-686, but it is unmarked.

To reach the southern end, take Va-634 from US-60. Park at Salt Log Gap, where Va-634 crosses the AT. Take the AT north for approximately 1.25 m. to intersection with the Railroad Trail, on the right.

Detailed trail data:

0–6.5 Unpaved road off Blue Ridge Parkway. This was formerly a railroad bed. Pass tank-trap blocking old railroad grade on right and go right at fork ahead.

.1–6.4 Turn right onto logging road and ascend. Bear left where former railroad bed intersects on right. Striped maple.

.2–6.3 Go left at triangle. Road to right is a new logging road. Level.

.8–5.7 Excellent view of the cleared Mill Creek hollow, Montebello, and the state fish hatchery.

.9–5.6 Go left at fork. Old timber cut.

1.4–5.1 Lots of yellow birch on the left.

1.5–5.0 Pass large, old, timber cut.

1.7–4.8 Bear right, up hill at fork.

1.8–4.7 Spring on right, just beyond boulder. Water should be boiled before use.

2.3–4.2 Possible campsite, down hill on left. Trail becomes shaded just ahead.

2.4–4.1 AT (south) intersects on right. Old road intersects on left. A few feet ahead, the trail forks. Left fork is the AT (north). Go right at fork. This is a pleasant, open area with a view down the valley of North Fork Piney River. In 50 yards, go straight through crossroad. The former railroad went to the right here. Good campsites are here. Descend. The trail becomes shaded and lined with ferns.

2.7–3.8 Hemlocks begin.

2.8–3.7 Turn right at junction. Good campsite on right under hemlocks. Cross a tributary of Elk Pond Branch just ahead.

3.0–3.5 Cross stream, ascend small hill, then descend again.

3.4–3.1 Cross Elk Pond Branch. Short, steep ascent just ahead.

3.6–2.9 Old trail intersects on right. Go left and descend.

3.8–2.7 Cross North Fork Piney River. Robert Rose, Henry Bruch, and John Blyre, on a four-day exploration trip in December 1749, passed this spot as they followed this creek to its source at Lovingston Spring. Ascend.

4.1–2.4 Level. This is an unusual right-angle junction between Wolf Ridge and a long ridge extending from Rocky Mtn. Descend just ahead.

4.8–1.7 Trail on right leads to a cabin on the hill. Do not trespass. Go left.

5.0–1.5 Old trail intersects on left. Go straight.

5.1–1.4 Cross intermittent stream.

5.4–1.1 Go right at fork.

5.5–1.0 Old trail intersects on right. Go straight.

6.5–0 Junction with AT. To the left, the AT (south) leads approximately 1.25 m. to Salt Log Gap. To the right, the AT (north) leads approximately 4.6 m. back to junction with Railroad Trail.

Straight ahead, the trail intersects the road that leads to the FAA radio towers on top of Rocky Mtn.

KING CREEK TRAIL

2.6 m. **PATC map #13: J-7**

This unblazed, unmaintained trail is actually Va-698; but it is difficult to imagine even a four-wheel-drive vehicle negotiating the rugged terrain. This trail provides access for bushwhackers who want to explore the abandoned, overgrown trails to The Cardinal and The Friar. It is no longer hikable on a circuit.

Access:

From US-60, turn onto Va-634. Turn right at second junction. Cross AT at Salt Log Gap. The route designation is Va-827 from the gap eastward. Trailhead is five miles east of gap, and is marked by a Forest Service sign on the right side of the road. There is room for two cars to park beside the road.

The southern end is on Va-629. There is no parking here.

Detailed trail data:

0–2.6 Forest Service sign on Va-827. Ascend very steeply on old road. Excellent campsite on left ahead. Hemlock, sassafras, and yellow poplar predominate.

.3–2.3 Rocky footing.

.4–2.2 Cross stream.

.6–2.0 Cross stream.

.9–1.7 Cross stream. Red maple and striped maple predominate in this upper section of the trail.

1.0–1.6 Cross-roads in a saddle. Trail to left leads to peak of The Friar, but becomes terribly overgrown after 300 yards. It is followable for those willing to bushwhack. Trail to right leads over The Cardinal, but is no longer passable after .9 m., except for those willing to do heavy bushwhacking. Descend steeply straight ahead.

1.3–1.3 Pass farm (no trespassing) and cross stream.

1.6–1.0 Cross stream.

1.8–.8 Cross stream.

1.9–.7 Cross King Creek.

2.3–.3 Pass farm (no trespassing).

2.5–.1 Cross King Creek.
2.6–0 Cross Little Piney River and end at intersection with Va-629.

FDR-48

3.1 m.   **PATC map #13: H-11**

Although lightly graveled for much of its length, this road is scenic and very useful for circuit hikes in conjunction with the AT. Robert Rose, Henry Bruch, and John Blyre, on a four-day exploration trip in December 1749, probably crossed this road as they traveled from Salt Log Gap to Pompey Mtn.

Access:

From US-60, turn onto Va-634. Turn right onto Va-755, which becomes FDR-48. Pass junction with FDR-520 and clearing beside former Wiggins Spring Shelter (now removed). Park at Hog Camp Gap, in lot with room for about six cars, on left just beyond the AT junction.

To reach the northern end, take Va-634 from US-60. Turn right at second junction. Park at Salt Log Gap, where AT crosses Va-634. FDR-48 intersects Va-634 on southern side of gap.

Detailed trail data:

0–3.1 Gate beside Hog Camp Gap parking. Lowland farmers formerly grazed their animals in these mountains, and this gap was used to round up the hogs at the end of summer. The slopes of Tar Jacket Ridge, at left, were largely bare ten years ago, but are now rapidly becoming reforested. Ahead, the road gives a good long-distance view of the mountains to the east. Descend.

.2–2.9 Two roads intersect on right; the second is FDR-51. Both lead to the Pompey Mtn.-Mt. Pleasant Loop Trail. Go straight.

.8–2.3 Lots of mountain laurel on right. Ascend ahead.

.9–2.2 Pass old timber cut on right. Notice treeline on ridge, which indicates an even older timber cut. Descend ahead.

1.5–1.6 Pass through dark hemlock grove. Good campsites on creek flats, down hill to left.

1.7–1.4 Junction with FDR-1167, on right, in large clearing. Ahead, cross south fork of Piney River, which runs under the road, and pass Piney River Trail (FDR-63A), an unmarked, disused road on right. Generally ascend ahead.

2.3–.8   Old road intersects on left. Go straight. Striped maple and American elm overwhelmingly predominate in vicinity.

3.1–0   Intersect AT and Va-634 at Salt Log Gap.

PINEY RIVER TRAIL (FDR-63A)

1.4 m.   **PATC map #13: H-10**

This unmarked, unmaintained, disused road parallels the south fork of Piney River. It will likely be too overgrown for use in summer, but it offers an alternate circuit in conjunction with the AT, FDR-48, and FDR-63 (the designation for Va-634/Va-827 within the Forest), which is a pleasant road despite occasional traffic.

Access:

The southern end is on FDR-48, 1.7 m. from Hog Camp Gap and 1.4 m. from Salt Log Gap.

The northern end is on FDR-63 (Va-634/Va-827), but no parking is possible there.

Detailed trail data:

0–1.4   Descend with many pleasant views of creek.

.3–1.1   Small cascade.

.6–.8   Turn right. The road on left comes to an end in a few yards.

.7–.7   Old road intersects on right. Turn left. The trail is very close to the creek here.

1.3–.1   Private residence on left. No trespassing.

1.4–0   Junction with FDR-63 (Va-634/Va-827). AT in Salt Log Gap is about 1.5 m. to left.

FDR-1167

3.5 m.   **PATC map #13: H-10**

Although graveled in places and still in use, this logging road offers a pleasant out-and-back hike. It also gives access to the overgrown trail that crosses The Cardinal, for experienced bushwhackers who want to explore that mountain. Several clearcuts offer views that are probably outstanding (judging from acoustical clues), but a dense fog during my scouting hike prevented me from verifying this. Only a portion of this dead-end road is presented here. Lack of time precluded a complete scouting.

Access:

This road begins on FDR-48, 1.7 m. from Hog Camp Gap and 1.4 m. from Salt Log Gap. The first .9 m. is drivable for most cars, but thereafter the road becomes very rough and dangerously narrow (only one lane) on a steep slope.

Detailed trail data:

0–3.5 Junction with FDR-48. Several cars can park in the clearing here. Level on wide, gravel road.

.1–3.4 Gate. Rhododendron, some quite large, lines the road.

.2–3.3 Ascend.

.7–2.8 Clearing. Old, overgrown road, blocked by tank-trap, intersects on right. Possible view from top of tank-trap. Lots of bindweeds and columbines here. Contrary to PATC map #13 (1985 ed.), the road follows the old Cardinal trail along the ridge from here.

.8–2.7 Old, overgrown road forks to right onto embankment. Go straight.

.9–2.6 Road forks to right and descends, sometimes steeply. Old, overgrown Cardinal trail, blocked by tank-trap, continues up ridge. A couple cars can park here.

1.4–2.1 Old road intersects on right. Bear left, staying on gravel.

1.8–1.7 Hairpin curve. Possible campsite in clearing on right. Cut log on right is virtually the only good place to sit on the whole road.

2.4–1.1 Clearcut with view on left.

2.6–.9 End of clearcut.

2.8–.7 Old road intersects on right (possible campsite). Just ahead, cross Little Piney River, which runs through a culvert under the road.

3.0–.5 Old road intersects on right. In 35 yards, an old, overgrown road forks to left. Keep to main road.

3.2–.3 Clearcut with view on left. Road blocked by tank-trap descends its left margin. Bear right and ascend.

3.3–.2 Clearcut on right, too.

3.4–.1 Descends briefly, then ascends.

3.5–0 End of clearcut. FDR-1167 is unscouted past this point. Ahead, it crosses Doefoot Mtn. and Georges Creek before dead-ending on Cardinal Ridge.

POMPEY MTN.-MT. PLEASANT LOOP

4.8 m.   **PATC map #13: H-11**

This blue-blazed, maintained trail was constructed by the Forest Service in 1980. It offers an easy, outstanding, circuit hike that encompasses two 4,000-foot mountains. Three portions of the trail are subject to heavy growth of grass, so great attention must be given to the dangers of snakes and ticks. A short spur trail (described separately below) leads to a spectacular view on Mt. Pleasant, whose summit is only one foot lower than Rocky Mtn., the highest mountain in the Pedlar District. This trail constitutes part of the Mt. Pleasant Special Management Area (see "Hiking in the Pedlar District").

Robert Rose, Henry Bruch, and John Blyre, on a four-day exploration trip in December 1749, crossed Pompey Mtn. from the source of Little Piney River to George's Creek. They then followed England Ridge down to Little Piney River.

A hike starting and ending at Hog Camp Gap, and including the Mt. Pleasant Spur Trail, is 6.1 m.

Access:

From US-60, turn onto Va-634. Turn right onto Va-755, which becomes FDR-48. Pass junction with FDR-520 and clearing beside former Wiggins Spring Shelter (now removed). Parking lot on left at Hog Camp Gap, just beyond the AT junction, has room for about six cars. Pass gate here and go .2 m. farther, then turn right at second intersecting road (FDR-51, the Forest extension of Va-635). In another .1 m., park off road at clearing with bulletin board.

Detailed trail data:

0–4.8 Bulletin board. Cross stile and ascend, steeply at first, then more gradually, hiking clockwise on loop. Ferns and some rhododendron line the trail.

.1–4.7 The next mile of trail is very grassy and apt to be overgrown some at times. An extensive growth of yellow evening primroses can be seen here.

.3–4.5 Ascend very steeply, then level ahead.

.5–4.3 Possible camp on right. Ascend, then level again.

.7–4.1 Descend. Possible camp by rock outcrop on right. Lots of bindweeds just ahead.

.9–3.9 Peak of Pompey Mtn. visible through trees on right.

1.1–3.7 Turn sharply right as old road curves away to left. *This is easy to miss*.

1.2–3.6 Turn left at junction. Level. Ascend through ferns ahead. Just ahead, a giant rhododendron forms a canopy over the trail.

1.5–3.3 Ascend steeply. More dead American chestnuts can be seen here than on any other trail in the Pedlar District. Giant oaks and yellow birch predominate.

1.6–3.2 Summit of Pompey Mtn. (4,032 feet). No view. The grass here sometimes gets high, and the trail may be obscure. Abundant ferns and rhododendron. Possible campsite.

1.8–3.0 Descend through thicket of mountain laurel and azalea.

2.2–2.6 Go left at fork onto a relocation. Trail on right rejoins loop in a little over .1 m. (at 2.5–2.3 m. mark).

2.3–2.5 Saddle. Very weedy and grassy. Trail may be obscure.

2.4–2.4 Junction with Mt. Pleasant Spur Trail, on left, which leads to spectacular summit in .3 m. To continue on loop, turn right.

2.5–2.3 Go left at fork and descend.

2.9–1.9 Cross intermittent stream.

3.1–1.7 Turn right at junction and cross stream in 70 yards.

3.3–1.5 Old, overgrown road intersects on left. Turn right. Ascend ahead.

3.5–1.3 Old road intersects on right. Go straight. In 70 yards, another old road intersects on right. Go straight, and then bear left where a third old road intersects on right.

3.6–1.2 Cross creek and ascend. Ahead, go straight when old road intersects on right.

3.7–1.1 Cross small stream and another just ahead. Pass through stand of elm saplings and hickory saplings with giant leaves.

3.9–.9 Former clearing is rapidly filling up with young locust trees and blackberry. Level.

4.3–.5 Ascend slightly.

4.7–.1 Cross tank-trap.

4.8–0 Cross stile and tank-trap and come to bulletin board at end of loop.

MT. PLEASANT SPUR TRAIL

.3 m.   PATC map #13: I-11

Access:

See description for Pompey Mtn.-Mt. Pleasant Loop.

Detailed trail data:

0–.3 From the junction at 2.4 m., go left on blue-blazed trail. Then go right at fork in 50 yards. Route to spring on left is usually overgrown badly in summer. Ascend very steeply. Rhododendron.

.3–0 Fork near summit. Left trail leads down mountain to private land. Right trail leads 50 yards to clearing for one tent and to summit on rocks. At an elevation of 4,071 feet, this is only one foot lower than Rocky Mtn., the highest mountain in the Pedlar District. The large, flat rocks and spectacular view make this an ideal location for lunch. The view comprises Chestnut Ridge (south), Bald Mtn. and Cole Mtn. (west), Tar Jacket Ridge (northwest), and Pompey Mtn. (north). The precipitous drop to the deep rift of the north fork of Buffalo River accentuates the feeling of great height. Rare peregrine falcons, an endangered species, nest in the vicinity and can sometimes be seen in flight.

FDR-51

3.5 m.   PATC map #13: I-13

This rough dirt road sustains little, if any, vehicular traffic below its upper end. It parallels the north fork of Buffalo River, and it provides an alternative means of access into this vicinity of the Forest.

Access:

From US-60, turn onto Va-635 at Forks of Buffalo. State maintenance ends at the Forest boundary, about 3.5 m. up. Thereafter, the road is designated FDR-51. There is no parking below the Forest boundary. Four-wheel-drive vehicles will find ample parking about .5 m. above the boundary.

The northern end intersects FDR-48 near Pompey Mtn.-Mt. Pleasant Loop.

Detailed trail data:

0–3.5 National Forest boundary. Cross Buffalo River and ascend. Northern red oak, striped maple, honeylocust, chestnut oak, and American chestnut shoots predominate along this road.

.5–3.0 Cross Buffalo River. There is parking here. The river is very scenic along here.

1.1–2.4 Cross Buffalo River.

1.2–2.3 Road intersects on right. This road leads up to Chestnut Ridge and Panther Mtn., but because "no trespassing" notices have turned it into a dead-end, it has not been included in this guide. Bear left.

2.0–1.5 Old road intersects on right. Bear left.

2.1–1.4 Cross Buffalo River. Possible campsite. Lots of yellow birch and ash.

2.2–1.3 Old road enters on left. Bear right.

2.3–1.2 Old road intersects on right. Bear left.

2.4–1.1 Good view on left of Little Rocky Mtn. and Floyd's Mtn.

2.8–.7 Old road intersects on left. Bear right.

3.0–.5 Old road intersects on right. Go straight and cross stream.

3.3–.2 Junction with Old Hotel Trail, on left.

3.4–.1 Junction with Pompey Mtn.-Mt. Pleasant Loop.

3.5–0 Junction with FDR-48. Hog Camp Gap is .2 m. to left.

OLD HOTEL TRAIL

3.2 m.   **PATC map #13: H-11**

This yellow-blazed trail, constructed and maintained by the Forest Service, opened to the public in 1989. One of the loveliest trails in the Pedlar District, it makes possible an outstanding circuit hike of moderate difficulty in conjunction with the AT over Cole (Cold) Mtn., which has the finest view in the Pedlar District. Named for a 19th-century resort planned for Cole Mtn.'s summit (but never built), this trail passes through a large mountainside meadow with a wonderful view and through a virgin hardwood forest along Little Cove Creek, all part of the Mt. Pleasant Special Management Area (see "Hiking in the Pedlar District").

Access:

See description for Pompey Mtn.-Mt. Pleasant Loop. From Loop trailhead, hike down FDR-51 for .1 m. to gate on right.

The trail's upper end intersects the AT at Cowcamp Gap, 1.9 m. from parking at Hog Camp Gap.

Detailed trail data:

0–3.2 Gate. Descend on old road through northern red oak, red maple, and hickory. In 70 yards, go straight as an old road intersects on right. Beyond, a stream briefly parallels the trail on left. This is the headwaters of Buffalo River's north fork.

.2–3.0 Ascend briefly.

.3–2.9 Descend. Virginia pine, some white pine.

.4–2.8 Good view of Mt. Pleasant, with its distinctive pointed peak and jagged rocks on one ridge, and of the bowl created by the North Fork valley. A cleared slope, 50 yards ahead, offers an even better, 180-degree view. Trail undulates ahead.

.6–2.6 Former clearcut, now partly regrown, affords view of valley and of hillside meadow ahead.

.7–2.5 Bear to right at fork and ascend, very steeply in places, passing a field of blackberries. Trail then curves back to left, along the length of the meadow. Not well marked; follow the track of the rutted road. Outstanding view throughout meadow.

.9–2.3 Spring emerges from under boulders 20 yards up slope on right. (Water from this untested source should be boiled before use.) Ahead, the trail bears left toward the trees on the ridge crest.

1.1–2.1 Excellent campsite in broad, flat, open area under a grove of old oaks on the ridge crest. On reaching grove, bear right off road and cross the crest while keeping treeline on left. On reaching young trees, bear right and descend on trail toward main ridge of Cole (Cold) Mtn. Ahead, a dense stand of young Virginia pines lines the trail. (From the grove, the old road to the left follows the ridge a short distance before dead-ending where a fence encloses the ridge on three sides. Farther on, the ridge divides and gives rise to two knolls, named Floyds Mtn. and Little Rocky Mtn.)

1.3–1.9 Cross intermittent headwaters of Rocky Branch. Just ahead, look backward for view of badly eroded cliff on Cole (Cold) Mtn. Pass old stone wall on left ahead. Continue to descend, sometimes steeply, on old road.

1.7–1.5 Generally ascend on path.

1.9–1.3 Bear left along ridge crest.

2.0–1.2 Turn right at junction. Descend, sometimes steeply, on old road lined with mountain laurel.

2.3–.9 Old road intersects on left (probably not visible in summer). Rock outcrops on right. Ascend.

2.5–.7 Cross Little Cove Creek. Yellow birch, red maple, and shagbark hickory predominate in hollow above creek crossing.

2.6–.6 Path on right crosses creek and leads to Cowcamp Gap Shelter, which sleeps four comfortably.

2.7–.5 Turn left at junction (blue-blazed trail on right leads back to shelter), 20 yards after passing Cowcamp Gap Spring, on left. (Water from this untested source should be boiled before use.)

3.2–0 Junction with AT. To right, summit of Cole (Cold) Mtn. is .9 m. and Hog Camp Gap is 1.9 m. To left, US-60 is 4 m.

FDR-520 (BUCK MTN. ROAD)

4.1 m. **PATC map #13: G-12**

This logging road, in conjunction with the AT, is very useful for circuit hikes over Bald Knob and Cole (Cold) Mtn., which has the finest view in the Pedlar District. It provides a much easier hiking route for half the distance than would be the case if one hiked out and back on the AT. A circuit hike starting and ending at Hog Camp Gap is 10.1 m.; one starting and ending at US-60 is 12.0 m.

Access:

From US-60, take Va-634 to fork. Go right onto Va-755, which becomes FDR-48. Pass junction with FDR-520 and clearing beside former Wiggins Spring Shelter (now removed). Park at Hog Camp Gap, in lot with room for about six cars, on left just beyond AT junction. Hike back down road for 1.0 m. to FDR-520.

To reach the southern end, park at Long Mtn. Wayside, on US-60, and hike north on the AT for .9 m.

Detailed trail data:

0–4.1 Gate, off Va-755/FDR-48.

.1–4.0 Profuse growth of appendaged waterleaf on left.

.2–3.9 Chestnut stumps on left and a few giant white pines on right.

.4–3.7 Go straight through cross-road. Private residence on right. No trespassing.

.6–3.5 Hillside on left is covered with oak fern.

1.0–3.1 Cross stream.

1.5–2.6 Stream runs under the road through a culvert. Ascend.

1.9–2.2 Old trail intersects on left. View of ridge straight ahead.

2.2–1.9 Slightly obstructed view to west. Level.

2.3–1.8 Summit of Buck Mtn. (3,360 feet), which is actually just an outlying ridge of Bald Knob. Descend.

3.3–.8 Abundant growth of striped maple.

3.5–.6 Obstructed westward view.

4.0–.1 Obstructed westward view.

4.1–0 Junction with AT. The AT leads north 5.0 m. to Hog Camp Gap, and south .9 m. to US-60.

STATON'S FALLS

.1 m. **PATC map #13: E-12**

Staton's Falls, also known as Lace Falls and Deadman's Falls, is one of the scenic highlights of the Pedlar District. It is composed of several falls and cascades, which when added together descend a great height. The interesting feature of Staton's Falls is not the height, however, but the distinctive zig-zag pattern of the series of falls.

From the road, a somewhat treacherous, rocky path leads steeply down the canyon for a short distance. Do not climb out onto the wet rocks; they are slippery and extremely dangerous. The falls become more interesting as one descends the canyon.

Access:

From US-60, take Va-605 to fork. Go right at fork onto Va-633. The falls are on the left, just before Va-633 crosses Staton's Creek. There is room for several cars to park in clearing on right.

PANTHER FALLS

.5 m.   **PATC map #13: E-17**

This waterfall is not as interesting as Crabtree Falls or Staton's Falls. The main attraction is the superb swimming hole directly below the falls. The depth at the center of the pool is 22.5 feet. Diving is possible from the surrounding boulders, but is extremely dangerous and should not be done, because the rock walls slope toward the center of the pool. One must always be careful of slippery and sharp rocks. The creek flats below the falls are lovely.

Access:

From US-60, take FDR-315, a good gravel road. Bear right at first fork. After 3.6 m., turn left at junction onto FDR-315A, marked by a sign. This ends at a large parking area, beyond which the gated road is closed.

Detailed trail data:

0–.5   Gate. Camping is allowed in the wildlife clearing opposite the parking lot. Descend road past gate.

.2–.3   Large, flat, hemlock-covered area beside Pedlar River. Formerly an overused camping area, these flats have regenerated a carpet of greenery since the Forest Service closed the area to campers several years ago. Continue straight ahead on trail, paralleling river.

.5–0   Panther Falls.

ROBERT'S CREEK CEMETERY

.4 m.   **PATC map #13: E-17**

This old cemetery has about a dozen markers. Many are nearly buried or obscured by trees. All of the markers are anonymous, except for a marble stone that says, "Leanna Coleman, wife of Paul

Pedlar River at Panther Falls

Lawhorne, March 2, 1868, March 4, 1917." Coleman Mtn., a couple miles south on FDR-315, was probably named for an ancestor of this woman.

Access:

See description for Panther Falls.

Detailed trail data:

    0–.4   Camping is allowed in the wildlife clearing opposite the parking lot. Walk back on FDR-315A.

    .2–.2   Pass another wildlife clearing on left.

    .3–.1   Pass timber cut on right.

    .4–0   Cemetery on left.

ELEPHANT MOUNTAIN TRAIL SYSTEM

This trail system comprises three trails constructed and maintained by the Forest Service: Reservoir Hollow Trail (blazed blue), Elephant Mtn. Trail (blazed yellow), and Indian Gap Trail (blazed blue). These trails can be hiked on a circuit with a variety of distances, depending on how much out-and-back hiking one wants to do. The simple loop—consisting of Reservoir Hollow Trail, part of Indian Gap Trail, and 1.2 m. of residential streets in Buena Vista— is 5.5 m. This can be lengthened to 7.7 m. by adding an out-and-back hike of Elephant Mtn. Trail, and increased to a maximum of 9.9 m. by adding an out-and-back hike of the upper portion of Indian Gap Trail.

Despite its proximity to the town of Buena Vista, this is an interesting trail system that features some beautiful flora and the ruins of two reservoirs. Among the wildlife seen on my 1988 rescouting hike were a deer, a woodchuck, and, on Elephant Mtn. Trail, a 2.5-foot-long timber rattlesnake.

It is safer to leave one's car on the residential streets of Buena Vista than alongside US-60, so the best place to begin a circuit is at the foot of Reservoir Hollow Trail.

Access:

To reach the foot of Reservoir Hollow Trail, turn onto US-501 from US-60 in Buena Vista. Turn left onto 13th Street, which eventually turns a block to the right and becomes 12th Street. At its end, turn right and park along Pine Road or by gate at end of Pine Road. Start hike from gate.

To reach the foot of Indian Gap Trail, turn onto US-501 from US-60 in Buena Vista. Turn left onto 21st Street and park at the end of the street.

To reach the upper end of Indian Gap Trail, park at a pullover on the south side of US-60, between the Blue Ridge Parkway and Buena Vista. Look for the emblematic-hiker sign beside the trail.

RESERVOIR HOLLOW TRAIL

2.5 m.   **PATC map #13: C-18**

Detailed trail data:

0–2.5 Gate at end of Pine Road, which continues as a gravel road that soon turns rough.

.1–2.4 Pass brick building and pistol shooting range.

.2–2.3 Cross creek and ascend generally.

.4–2.1 Cross creek. Note that sedimentary strata in creek bed are tilted vertically. Common hoptree, yellow poplar, red maple, and beech ahead.

.6–1.9 Cross tiny stream and go right at fork; then, in 50 feet, go left at fork onto trail off road. Ascend steeply.

.7–1.8 Pass Forest Service fence, which marks start of trail as described in Forest Service brochure. Down hill to right is an old, overgrown reservoir, one of two that formerly stored water for Buena Vista. Depending on rainfall, reservoir may be filled or empty. Ahead, trail passes outcrop cliff on left and undulates through chestnut oak, hickory, river birch, mountain laurel, and rhododendron.

.9–1.6 Ascend.

1.0–1.5 Cross creek, then cross it again in 90 yards.

1.1–1.4 Cross creek.

1.3–1.2 Cross creek and ascend steeply through white pine and pitch pine.

1.7–.8 View of Elephant Mtn. on left. Trail becomes very steep.

1.8–.7 Good view of Paxton Peak, Reservoir Hollow and the Shenandoah Valley. The trail becomes very rocky.

2.0–.5   Junction with Elephant Mtn. Trail, on left. To continue on Reservoir Hollow Trail, go right at fork. Level ahead. Rhododendron.

2.1–.4   Ascend. Possible campsites along here. Abundant young chestnut, dogwood, and mountain laurel.

2.2–.3   Descend easily at first, then more steeply along ravine.

2.4–.1   Abundant rhododendron.

2.5–0   Junction with Indian Gap Trail. Left fork leads to Buena Vista. Right fork leads to US-60.

ELEPHANT MOUNTAIN TRAIL

1.1 m.   **PATC map #13: C-18**

Detailed trail data:

0–1.1   Junction with Reservoir Hollow Trail. Ascend through pitch pine.

.1–1.0   Level. Lots of rhododendron, mountain laurel, and azalea here and at many other points on trail. Ahead, descend steeply with view of Elephant Mtn. peak.

.3–.8   Level in saddle. Possible campsite. Ascend over small knoll ahead. Young chestnuts.

.5–.6   Paxton Peak can be seen from viewpoint on left. Descend very steeply to narrow saddle, then ascend.

.6–.5   Knoll. Descend very steeply to saddle, then ascend.

.7–.4   Knoll. Descend very steeply to saddle, then ascend very steeply. Good views when leaves are down.

1.1–0   Trail ends on wooded summit of Elephant Mtn. (2,101 feet). Although the path continues beyond this point, its outlet is on private land and so should not be hiked.

INDIAN GAP TRAIL

3.0 m.   **PATC map #13: D-17**

The first half-mile of this trail does not follow the route shown on the 1985 edition of PATC map #13 and on the Forest Service brochure of the Elephant Mtn. Trail System. Instead, it curves around a knoll slightly to the west.

Detailed trail data:

0–3.0 Emblematic-hiker sign on US-60.

.1–2.9 Cross stream and ascend steeply through hemlock, river birch, and elm.

.2–2.8 Ascend more easily through generally open forest of chestnut oak.

.3–2.7 Mountain laurel.

.8–2.2 Unmaintained path intersects on left. It ascends slightly through a wide hollow in which chestnut oak overwhelmingly predominates, and reaches the Blue Ridge Parkway in .2 m. at a point 150 feet south of the Indian Gap parking area.

1.1–1.9 Junction with Reservoir Hollow Trail, on left. To continue on Indian Gap Trail, bear right. Descend with rocky footing through thick growth of rhododendron.

1.3–1.7 Descend very steeply with treacherous footing. Rhododendron ends and profuse growth of hemlock begins.

1.5–1.5 Trail enters end of very old road. Descent is less steep from here, and footing improves.

1.6–1.4 Good campsite under hemlocks on right.

1.7–1.3 Cross Indian Gap Run. Trail becomes path again and parallels powerline from here on. Timber regeneration area.

2.0–1.0 Cross creek.

2.1–.9 Cross creek. Cardinal flowers. In next 140 yards, cross creek twice more, with cardinal flowers and thick undergrowth beside trail.

2.2–.8 Cross creek and enter old road again. Apparently the interruption in this old road is because it has been washed out by the creek.

2.4–.6 Thick growth of smooth false foxglove flowers. In 90 yards, cross creek with view of rockslide on right and more cardinal flowers; then cross creek again in another 70 yards.

2.5–.5 Stone wall with gate on right. On the other side are the overgrown ruins of a dam and reservoir, one of two that formerly stored water for Buena Vista. Spotted touch-me-not (jewelweed) flowers, good for poison ivy, are just ahead.

2.6–.4 Cross creek and pass old quarry in side of hill.

2.7–.3 Go right at fork and pass through a former clay quarry, now part of the undeveloped Laurel Park, a city property.

3.0–0 End of 21st Street in Buena Vista. To reach Reservoir Hollow Trail, turn left onto Cedar Avenue. Turn left onto 12th Street, then turn right onto Pine Road after two blocks. Distance is 1.2 m.

INDIAN ROCKS TRAIL

.1 m.   PATC map #13: D-17

This trail, part of the Blue Ridge Parkway, is administered by the National Park Service. It is not part of the Pedlar District, but because it is surrounded by the district, and because it is interesting, it is included in this guide.

The trail ends at a pile of large, columnar rocks. There is no view, but the rock formations are fascinating. For example, it is possible to walk upright for five yards under a column balanced between two rocks. The shaded, flat tops of many boulders provide an ideal site for lunch.

Access:

From US-60, go south on the Blue Ridge Parkway. Park at the Indian Gap parking area.

DANCING CREEK-BROWN'S CREEK TRAIL

6.3 m.   PATC map #13: I-23

Access:

From US-60, take Va-635 south. Turn right onto Va-610 .25 m. past Pleasant View. Follow Va-610 past Va-641 and Va-607, then over Dancing Creek. Trailhead is on right about .25 m. past the creek. There is room for two cars to park here.

From Va-130, take Va-610 north to trailhead on left.

It is also possible to park at the Dancing Creek overlook, on the Blue Ridge Parkway between US-60 and Va-130, and hike south on the parkway for .3 m. to its crossing with the trail.

Detailed trail data:

0–6.3 Junction with Va-610.

.1–6.2 Cemetery on left. Some of the markers are chiseled stone (including "Wood, 1896" and "Downey, 1889"), and some are

Natural ladder up Spy Rock

carved wooden planks ("Noel, 1907"). A few of the stones have intricate, stylized flower designs. Many stones are anonymous. The most recent stone is "Downey, 1915."

.5–5.8   View of Big Piney Mtn. on right.

.7–5.6   A gas pipeline parallels the trail closely on the left.

1.0–5.3   Cross pipeline.

1.3–5.0   Cross pipeline.

1.5–4.8   Cross pipeline.

1.6–4.7   Trail intersects on left. Go straight.

1.8–4.5   Red gate at junction with Blue Ridge Parkway. Cross parkway and ascend.

2.0–4.3   Good view of surrounding mountains: Peavine Mtn., Silas Knob, and Bluff Mtn. Descend.

2.2–4.1   Two old roads intersect on left in rapid succession. Go straight, then around curve to right. Do not cross creek. Ascend.

2.5–3.8   Trail intersects on left. Bear right.

2.9–3.4   Good view on right over low scrub trees.

3.0–3.3   Trail intersects on left. Go right and cross pipeline. Descend ahead.

3.2–3.1   Go left at fork. Ascend.

3.7–2.6   Trail intersects on left. Keep right.

4.2–2.1   Trail intersects on left. Go straight.

4.5–1.8   Overgrown trail intersects on left. Go sharply to right and descend.

4.6–1.7   Overgrown trail intersects on left. A possible campsite is here. Yellow poplar is profuse. Bear right. Trail becomes very wet and rocky. Lots of hemlock.

4.7–1.6   Trail goes under a Blue Ridge Parkway overpass. The trail is covered with two inches of water after a period of no rain; it would certainly be impassable after a heavy rain.

5.0–1.3   Cross Brown's Creek and ascend.

5.8–.5   Level.

5.9–.4   Ascend short distance, then descend steeply.

6.3–0   Cross Enchanted Creek and intersect Va-607.

BELLE COVE TRAIL

4.7 m.   **PATC map #13: B-22**

This blue-blazed trail, constructed and maintained by the Forest Service, is one of the most beautiful in the Pedlar District. Those who do not care to hike the entire trail are fortunate in that the first half, which passes through a narrow canyon, is the most scenic. The footing is generally very good, and the 1,700-foot ascent is so gradual as to be extremely easy.

Access:

The trail, on US-501 between Buena Vista and Glasgow, is marked by an emblematic-hiker sign. The highway crossing of Belle Cove Branch is also marked by a sign that names the creek. There is room for about five cars to park. Do not block the dirt road.

The eastern end of the trail intersects the AT at Saltlog Gap.

Detailed trail data:

0–4.7 Gate on old road. Ascend slightly.

.1–4.6 Pass eastern red cedar, eastern redbud, and bindweed.

.2–4.5 Old trail intersects on left.

.3–4.4 Go right at fork, and then turn left off dirt road onto a more overgrown road. Mileage sign and white pine are here.

.5–4.2 Possible camp on right. Yellow poplar, red maple, silver maple, and several varieties of oak. Cross intermittent stream ahead.

.9–3.8 Belle Cove Branch on right. This was nearly dry during a summer drought.

1.0–3.7 Trail has eroded to become dry creekbed. Hemlock growth begins here.

1.1–3.6 Cross creek in a beautiful spot. Cliff on left. In 70 yards, cross creek and ascend more steeply with overhanging cliff on right.

1.2–3.5 Wading pool on right.

1.3–3.4 Cross creek. View of rockslide on left.

1.5–3.2 Descend.

1.7–3.0 Cross creek. Generally level.

1.8–2.9 Rockslide on right.

1.9–2.8 Lots of rhododendron.

2.1–2.6 Ascend.

2.2–2.5 Descend and cross creek in very narrow, interesting defile.

2.3–2.4 Cross creek and ascend slightly. Ahead, pass superb wading pool on left.

2.4–2.3 Cross creek.

2.5–2.2 Bear to left with rocky footing. Do not cross creek. This is very badly marked.

2.6–2.1 Cross creek.

2.7–2.0 Trail has eroded into creek. In 50 yards, cross creek.

2.8–1.9 Cross creek. Lots of rhododendron ahead.

3.1–1.6 River birch, hickory, sycamore, and hemlock predominate.

3.2–1.5 Cross creek and ascend more steeply.

3.3–1.4 Level. Possible camp on left in beautiful open forest.

3.4–1.3 Cross intermittent stream and ascend.

3.7–1.0 Open forest ends. Cross intermittent stream.

3.8–.9 Trail begins to ascend by long switchbacks.

4.3–.4 Lots of shagbark hickory.

4.7–0 Intersect AT at Saltlog Gap, a flat field of high weeds. Possible campsite. Mileage sign. Saddle Gap Trail is 1.0 m. to right.

ROCKY ROW TRAIL

2.7 m. **PATC map #13: D-27**

This blue-blazed trail, constructed and maintained by the Forest Service, makes a steep, 1,200-foot ascent of Little Rocky Row, a narrow ridge. It offers several outstanding views of the James River gorge. The footing is generally good. Unfortunately, the trail cannot be hiked on any circuit, and it is questionable whether the views justify an out-and-back hike.

Access:

Midway between Glasgow and Snowden on Va-130 (also US-501), a George Washington National Forest sign that says "Bluff Mtn. 8" marks the beginning of this trail. Parking is available at a state historical marker pullover that is 150 yards southeast of the trailhead.

Detailed trail data:

0–2.7 Ascend through pine.

.2–2.5 Level.

.4–2.3   Lots of young chestnut oaks and sassafras. Ascend steeply.

.5–2.2   Cross powerline clearing. Excellent view.

.6–2.1   Ascend by long switchbacks.

1.0–1.7   This section is subject to heavy growth of weeds. Be careful of snakes. Trail is relatively level.

1.1–1.6   A short section of trail is obscured by weeds here. Follow the ridge. An excellent view of Glasgow on left.

1.5–1.2   Pass through a large variety of oaks, including the unusual blackjack oak.

1.6–1.1   Ascend steeply.

1.7–1.0   Pass prominent boulder. View of James River on right.

1.8–.9   Outstanding view of James River and the mountains beyond.

1.9–.8   Descend.

2.0–.7   Ascend.

2.2–.5   Wild geraniums. Descend ahead.

2.3–.4   Ascend slightly.

2.4–.3   Level. Excellent view of James River all along here. Lots of wild geraniums. Descend ahead.

2.5–.2   Ascend.

2.7–0   Junction with AT. To right, Johns Hollow Shelter is 1.4 m., and Va-130/US-501 is 3.2 m. To left, Saddle Gap Trail is 2.6 m., and Belle Cove Trail is 3.6 m.

SADDLE GAP TRAIL

2.5 m.   **PATC map #13: F-24**

This blue-blazed trail, recently reopened, uses the name and the upper portion of a long-abandoned trail that once served as the original AT route. However, the original Saddle Gap Trail ascended a parallel hollow somewhat south of the present route. Unfortunately, the 1985 PATC map shows the old route. Although this trail has only one narrow view near the top, it makes possible a splendid 9.0 m. circuit hike in conjunction with the AT and the quarry access road (Va-812).

Access:

About .75 m. west of the US-501/Va-130 junction, turn onto a disused industrial road (Va-812) opposite a boat landing and paralleling Rocky Row Run. Although paved, this road has many deep, treacherous potholes and fallen stones from the adjacent cliff, so special caution should be exercised. Follow this road about 2.5 m. to its end at the gate of the closed Hercules Co. quarry (no trespassing). There is room for two cars to park off the road here (do not block gate). (Another couple cars can park where the AT crosses this road.) Hike back 335 yards (.19 m.) to curve in road. The greenery on the hillside on right is cut away here, but the trailhead, behind a large tank-trap covered with blackberries, is still hard to find.

The northern end is on the AT at Saddle Gap.

Detailed trail data:

0–2.5 Cross large tank-trap, one of several in the lower end, and enter woods. Many blazes on this trail are on rocks. Ascend ahead on wide, old logging road.

.3–2.2 Old road intersects on right (a fork in reverse). Go straight and cross tank-trap and small stream just ahead.

.4–2.1 Go left at fork and ascend steeply.

.5–2.0 Bear left as faint old road intersects on right. Ascend gently. Ahead the trail becomes very weedy. Watch for snakes.

.6–1.9 Go left at fork and, in a few yards, bear to right and ascend. A small stream mingles with the trail at places ahead. In 90 yards, bear left with old wall briefly on right. Interesting flora, including cardinal flowers.

.7–1.8 Go right at fork. Bad weeds end.

.8–1.7 Ascend steeply, then very steeply.

.9–1.6 Go right at fork.

1.0–1.5 Go right at fork. Ahead, the trail levels off briefly, then becomes very steep again. In 70 yards, go left at fork.

1.1–1.4 Go left at fork.

1.2–1.3 Go right at fork.

1.3–1.2 Go straight at cross-roads and ascend a little less steeply.

1.4–1.1 Turn left, off road and onto path, ascending the steep hillside on a switchback. *This is easy to miss*! Note that cut-off occurs just after road begins to descend. Trail now ascends by a series of six long switchbacks.

2.3–.2 Slight, but nice, view.

2.5–0 Junction with AT in Saddle Gap. To left, Rocky Row Trail is 2.6 m. and quarry road (Va-812) is 4.6 m. To right, Belle Cove Trail in Saltlog Gap is 1.0 m.

PEAVINE MOUNTAIN TRAIL

5.0 m.   **PATC map #13: I-24**

Extensive clearcutting south of Peavine Mtn. and in the Terrapin Creek vicinity has largely wiped out all but one of the unofficial bushwhacking trails in this area, described in the first edition of this guide and depicted on the 1985 edition of PATC map #13. The exception is this unmarked trail, called "East Peavine Mtn. Trail" in the previous edition and on the 1985 PATC map. Although it is a logging road recently in use, it still offers an interesting hike. It leads through a maze of old roads to an artificial pond on the flat, wooded, southern summit of Peavine Mtn. Along the way, a great many toads, some of extraordinary size, may be seen in summer (do not touch them, however, for they excrete an irritating poison). Several mining operations were active in the area as recently as 1973, and it appears that all the water sources are consequently polluted with oil.

Access:

From Va-130, go 1.5 m. north on Va-610. Look for dirt road with gate on left. There is room for several cars to park beside the road.

Another possibility is to go 1.5 m. north on the Blue Ridge Parkway from Va-130. Park at Middle Otter Creek overlook. Hike .5 m. north to where the parkway crosses over this trail. Descend to trail from left side of Parkway.

Detailed trail data:

0–5.0 Gate on Va-610. Descend through red maple, white pine, beech, northern red oak, post oak, yellow poplar, and sassafras.

.3–4.7 Level.

.4–4.6 Cross Otter Creek. Ahead, pass under the Blue Ridge Parkway overpass. Ascend slightly, then level.

.6–4.4 Old road intersects on left. Go right at fork and cross stream. Lots of cardinal flowers, sugar maple, and hemlock.

1.1–3.9 Cross stream.

1.2–3.8 Old road intersects on left. Go straight.

1.3–3.7 Overgrown road straight ahead. Bear right, cross stream, and ascend.

1.5–3.5 Go straight at cross-roads, descend, then ascend again. Old clearcut on right.

1.6–3.4 Descend. Old clearcut on left.

1.8–3.2 Cross stream and ascend through profuse yellow poplar.

1.9–3.1 Old clearcuts on both sides ahead.

2.2–2.8 Ascend slightly, then level again.

2.4–2.6 Ascend steeply.

2.7–2.3 Old road intersects on left. It leads down to an old clearcut. Go straight.

2.8–2.2 View of nameless knob on left. This trail will pass to the northwest of that knob through a saddle between the knob and Peavine Mtn.

3.4–1.6 Descend.

3.5–1.5 Cross-road in clearing. The road that goes straight ahead does not appear on any map. The road to the right leads to the Blue Ridge Parkway, but is impassable after 300 yards. Turn left and descend through yellow poplar.

3.7–1.3 Ascend and bear right at fork.

3.9–1.1 Five-way fork in saddle between Peavine Mtn. and a nameless knob. The first trail on the left skirts the edge of the nameless knob. The second and third trails from the left form a single loop around the top of the knob. The fourth trail from the left is the old Cashaw Creek Trail, which becomes terribly overgrown after .6 m. The Cashaw Creek Trail is followable, but presents dangerous hiking because of the danger of snakes and ticks in the high grass. Ascend steeply on the fifth trail, on the immediate right.

4.0–1.0 Old road intersects on left. Bear right.

4.3–.7 Turn left and ascend steeply at cross-road. The road straight ahead leads to Peavine Gap. The overgrown road on the right leads to the Blue Ridge Parkway.

4.4–.6 Bear right at fork.

4.5–.5 Descend.

4.6–.4 Old road intersects on left. Go straight and descend. Ahead, pass old mine or timber cut on left and ascend.

4.7–.3 Level. Artificial pond the size of a football field is on right. This water is stagnant. It is not recommended for drinking or swimming.

4.8–.2 Excellent campsite 30 yards to right at fork. Bear left at fork. Ascend slightly ahead.

5.0–0 Superb campsite on left. This is the best campsite on the mountain. The large, wooded plateau that forms the southern summit of Peavine Mtn. (1,960 feet) has no views, but it appears to be a popular camping site. This trail continues down the mountainside, but is unexplored past this point.

OTTER CREEK TRAIL SYSTEM

This trail system is administered by the National Park Service. It is not part of the Pedlar District, but because it is surrounded by the District, and because it affords exceptional hiking, it is included in this guide. A map of the entire trail system can be found at the end of the southern-most parking lot at Otter Creek Recreation Area. An out-and-back hike of the entire system is 7.6 m. long.

Access:

From Va-130, take the Blue Ridge Parkway north to Otter Creek Recreation Area. A campground, restaurant, rest rooms, telephone, and gas station are here. Park at the end of the southern-most parking lot. Otter Creek Trail begins beside the map of the trail system.

Parts of the trail system can also be reached from Terrapin Hill overlook, Lower Otter Creek overlook, Otter Lake overlook, and the Otter Creek Visitor Center.

OTTER CREEK TRAIL

3.4 m.   PATC map #13: I-25

Detailed trail data:

0–3.4 Trail system map at Otter Creek Recreation Area.

.1–3.3 Take left trail across creek, then keep right, parallel to the creek. There are many transient trails in this area.

.2–3.2 Keep straight on main trail. A smaller path leads right, closer to the creek. White pine and mountain laurel on left just ahead.

.3–3.1 Pass under Blue Ridge Parkway bridge. This is completely dry after a period of little rain, but it could be difficult to cross in wet weather. Lots of lady fern along here.

.4–3.0 Bench beside interesting giant hemlock that is clinging sideways on the bank of the creek.

.5–2.9 Upward view of cliff on right.

.6–2.8 Stairs to Terrapin Hill overlook on left. Go straight. Ahead, pass through a lovely area of profuse hemlock.

.7–2.7 Pass under two bridges 100 yards apart.

.8–2.6 Cross creek on right over artificial stepping stones. Very interesting cliffs overhang Otter Creek just a few yards downstream. The 1985 edition of PATC map #13 is incorrect; it does not show this creek crossing. Just ahead, cross creek on left over artificial stepping stones. The trail is very vague here.

.9–2.5 Ascend steeply.

1.0–2.4 Bench. Another bench is 70 yards ahead.

1.1–2.3 Cross deep ravine, and pass giant hemlocks.

1.2–2.2 Bench. Descend.

1.3–2.1 Cross deep ravine over a very narrow bridge with handrails. Great care should be exercised here.

1.4–2.0 Cross deep ravine, then descend.

1.5–1.9 Cross ravine. Bench on left under impressive overhanging rocks. Descend steeply.

1.6–1.8 Trail parallels Otter Creek closely again. Climb up to left over large roots. The footing is bad here.

1.7–1.7 Bench.

1.8–1.6 Scramble over rocks.

1.9–1.5 Cross creek over artificial stepping stones.

2.0–1.4 Cross creek over artificial stepping stones.

2.2–1.0 Bench.

2.4–1.0 Junction with Otter Lake Loop Trail. Go right at fork. Strictly speaking, this is part of the Loop Trail, but for simplicity of classification this section is included as part of the Creek Trail. Ahead, cross narrow footbridge with rail over stream, then another over creek. Otter Lake, a man-made lake constructed by the Park

Service, is on the left. Swimming, boating, ice skating, and fishing are prohibited.

2.7–.7 Dam and waterfall. Keep off dam. Go left, down the stairs, at the trail sign. Then go straight. The Otter Lake Loop Trail goes to the left over the creek.

2.9–.5 Cross creek over artificial stepping stones. Notice the solid shale creek bottom.

3.0–.4 Cross creek over artificial stepping stones.

3.1–.3 Impressive cliffs on left.

3.3–.1 A short side-trail leads left to a view of a cliff that overhangs the creek.

3.4–0 Visitor Center at end of trail. This is a small, wooden pavilion. It has rest rooms, a water fountain, and exhibits on the history of the James River Canal. Between 1710 and 1720, the earliest settler in this area, a trader named Hughes, established a trading station near here.

CANAL LOCK TRAIL

.2 m.   PATC map #13: I-27

This trail leads to some restored locks of the James River Canal.

Detailed trail data:

0–.2 Go down stairs from Visitor Center. Ahead, Trail of the Trees branches to the right. The Canal Lock Trail goes left over a wide, concrete, pedestrian bridge, with metal railings, over James River.

.1–.1 Trail intersects on right. Go straight.

.2–0 Battery Creek locks and exhibits.

TRAIL OF THE TREES

.3 m.   PATC map #13: I-27

This is a superb nature trail. It has an amazing variety of trees, with plaques that identify each one. Included are the rare paw-paw, blackgum, yellow poplar, black walnut, sweetgum, red cedar, witchhazel, American sycamore, and many types of oaks, maples, and hickories.

Detailed trail data:

0–.3 Go right from junction with Canal Lock Trail. In 35 yards, loop trail begins. Go left and pass overlook of James River.

.1–.2 Cross wooden bridge. Ahead, pass James River overlook and continue straight up hill, not on the path that goes to the left.

.2–.1 Cross wooden bridge over ravine.

.3–0 The trail that goes to the left leads a few yards to a tiny cemetery. "Peters, 1919," has a nice carving of a mansion in marble. "Putt, 1878," is carved on slate. The other tombstones are anonymous. Ahead, reach junction with Canal Lock Trail.

OTTER LAKE LOOP TRAIL

.6 m.   **PATC map #13: I-27**

Detailed trail data:

0–.6 Cross Otter Creek over artificial stepping stones at the trail fork by the Otter Creek dam. Ahead, an interesting rock overhangs trail.

.1–.5 Bench.

.2–.4 Cross ravine, then ascend.

.3–.3 Bench. A side-trail goes to the left to an overlook that is 150 feet above the lake.

.4–.2 Bench. Descend into ravine.

.5–.1 Cross small stream. Ahead, cross wooden bridge with rail over stream.

.6–0 Pass ruins of log cabin and stone chimney in an overgrown clearing surrounded by beautiful white pines, and then reach junction with Otter Creek Trail.

The Potomac Appalachian Trail Club
1718 N Street, N.W.
Washington, D.C. 20036
Telephone 202/638-5306

This GUIDE is published by the Potomac Appalachian Trail Club. The Club is a volunteer group whose main purpose is the preservation and maintenance of a section of the Appalachian Trail. The Club is also responsible for a variety of maps, other publications, hiking and climbing, ski-touring excursions, and other activities. The Club Headquarters is open weekdays, 7 p.m. to 9:30 p.m., and Thursdays and Fridays, 11 a.m. to 2 p.m., except holidays. Visitors and callers are welcome.

In a Guide such as this it is inevitable that errors, both typographical and factual, will occur. Please report any you find to the editor, in care of PATC, so that they may be corrected in future editions.

The Potomac Appalachian Trail Club expressly denies any liability for any accident or injury to persons using these trails.